The images in this book:

All of the illustrations have been taken from a collection held by the U.S. Library of Congress (LoC). Their collection numbers a little over 2600 prints (and coloured slides of each) which covers a period of nearly 300 years up to 1915. The originals were made using the woodblock printing process and some of the finest examples of Japanese art and print-making are included in this period. We have selected about one-third of the collection of warrior prints for this book.

Copyright on the original art work?

None. The prints are in the public domain.

Copyright on this book and on the prints in it?

The book as a whole is copyright and may not be copied without the permission of the senior author. The prints in the book may be copied (recognizing they have been adjusted in many cases for size and quality). Acknowledgment of the source (LoC) is expected and reference to this book would be a courtesy.

More than just prints of brave Warriors?

There is a detailed history of the role of the warrior in Japanese culture, politics, and daily life in Wikipedia. As well, there are excellent sections on the philosophy of the warrior, on his conduct in battle and on his shift to the largely ceremonial role he now plays in contemporary society. In this collection you will find that the warrior is presented in almost every conceivable role and situation. You will find him among other representations as proud warrior, seducer, slayer of dragons , buffoon and youthful novice. He is shown engaging in formal duels and also as a bully ransacking humble dwellings and whereas at times he seems to be challenging the world, at other times he is seen hanging on to a cliff's edge, beaten by the elements.

Although the warrior typically occupied a high social status, artists were obviously not universally kind to them when it came to rendering these prints.

Those who created these images were, we believe, master artists and masters of their craft. The technique of creating a 'simple' black and white woodblock print involves cutting away all of the unused (or white) space in an image, then inking the remaining wood (a relief image) and pressing the paper or cloth onto it. To create a multi-colour image such as those seen in this book a series of blocks had to be prepared, one for each colour and the paper or cloth precisely pressed to each block so that edges and contours lined up as they should.

We hope you will enjoy the images as a whole – but do take the time to look at the detail, too.

David Abbey
Guelph, Ontario, Canada

Denise Abbey
Nanaimo, British Columbia, Canada

January, 2015

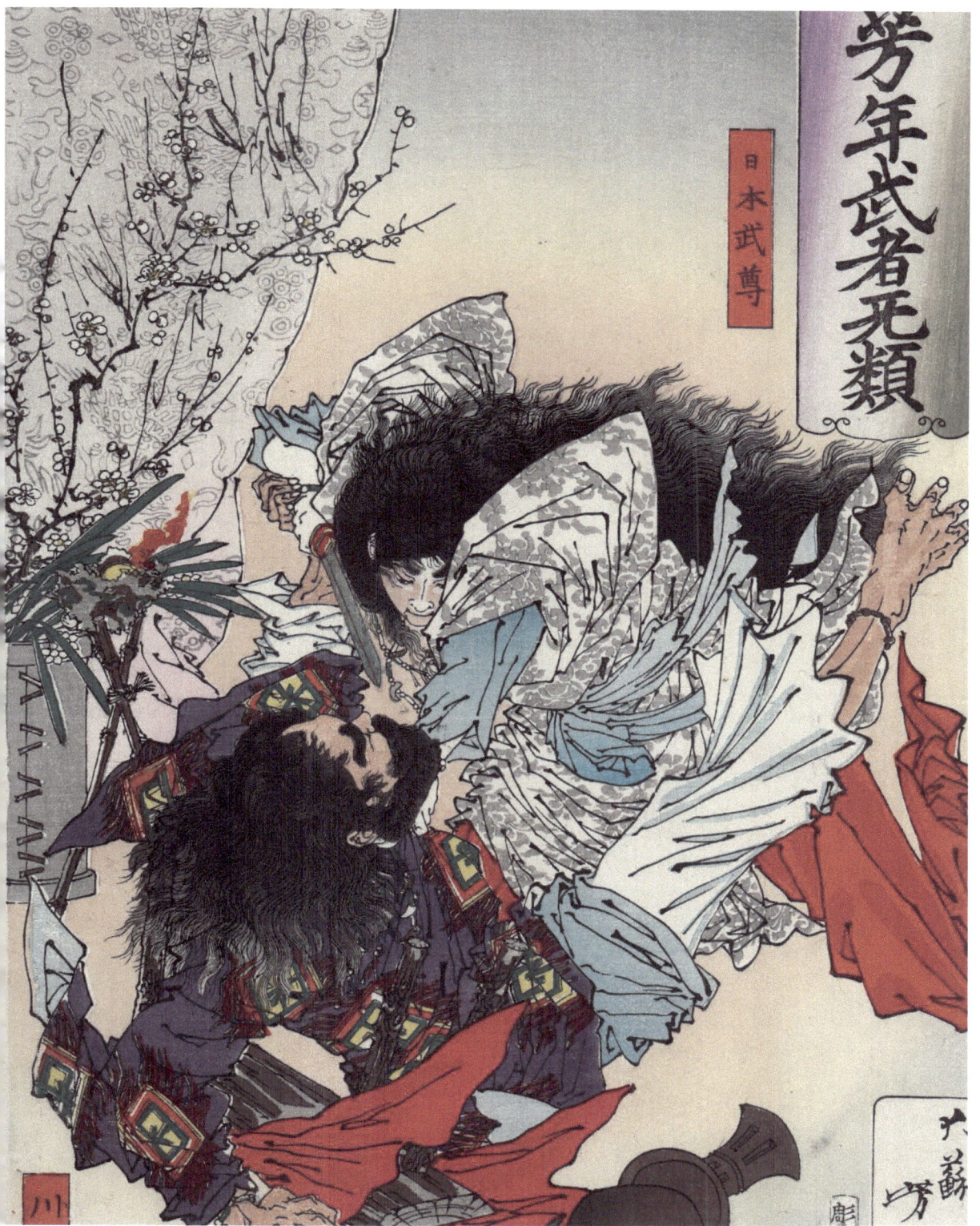

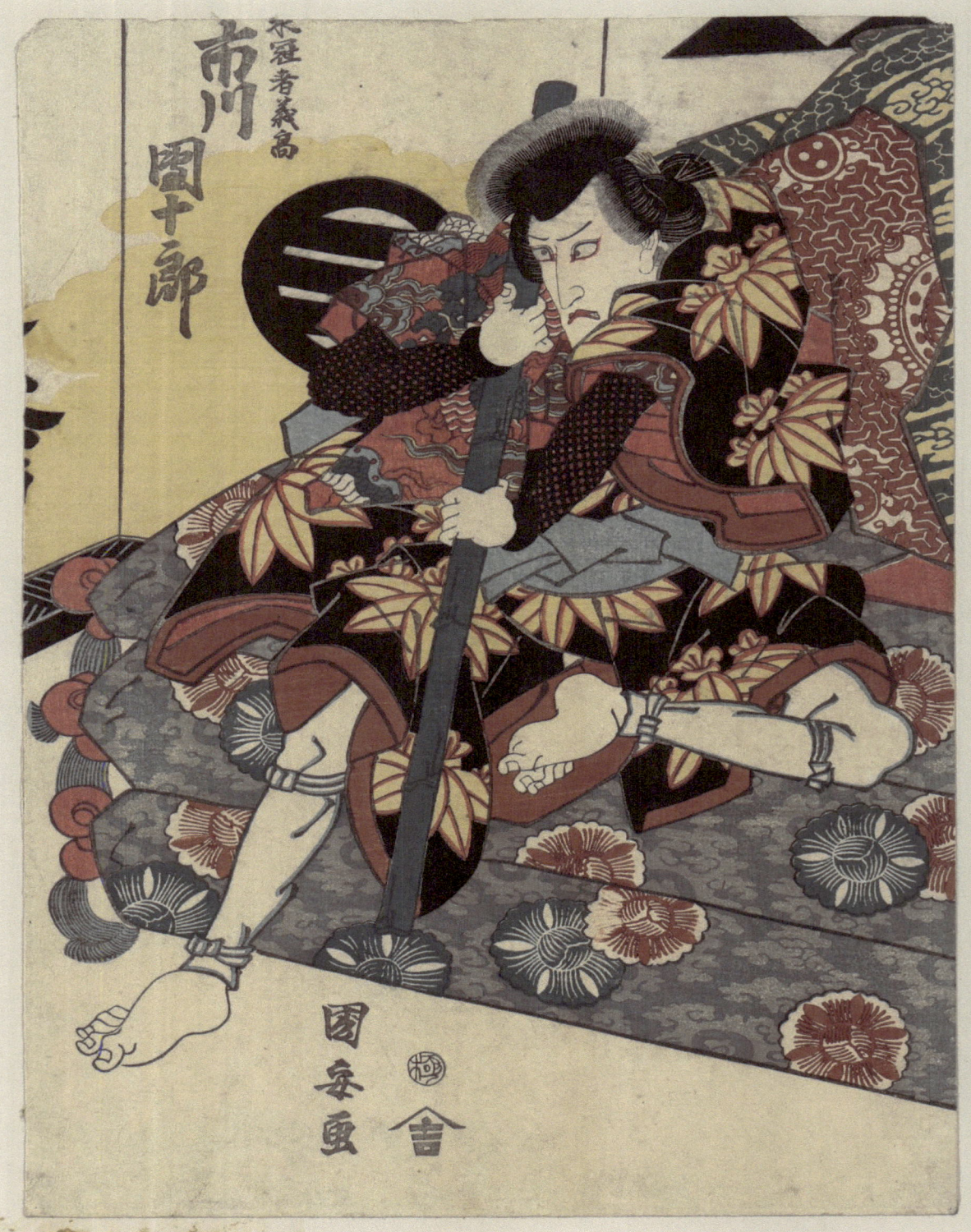

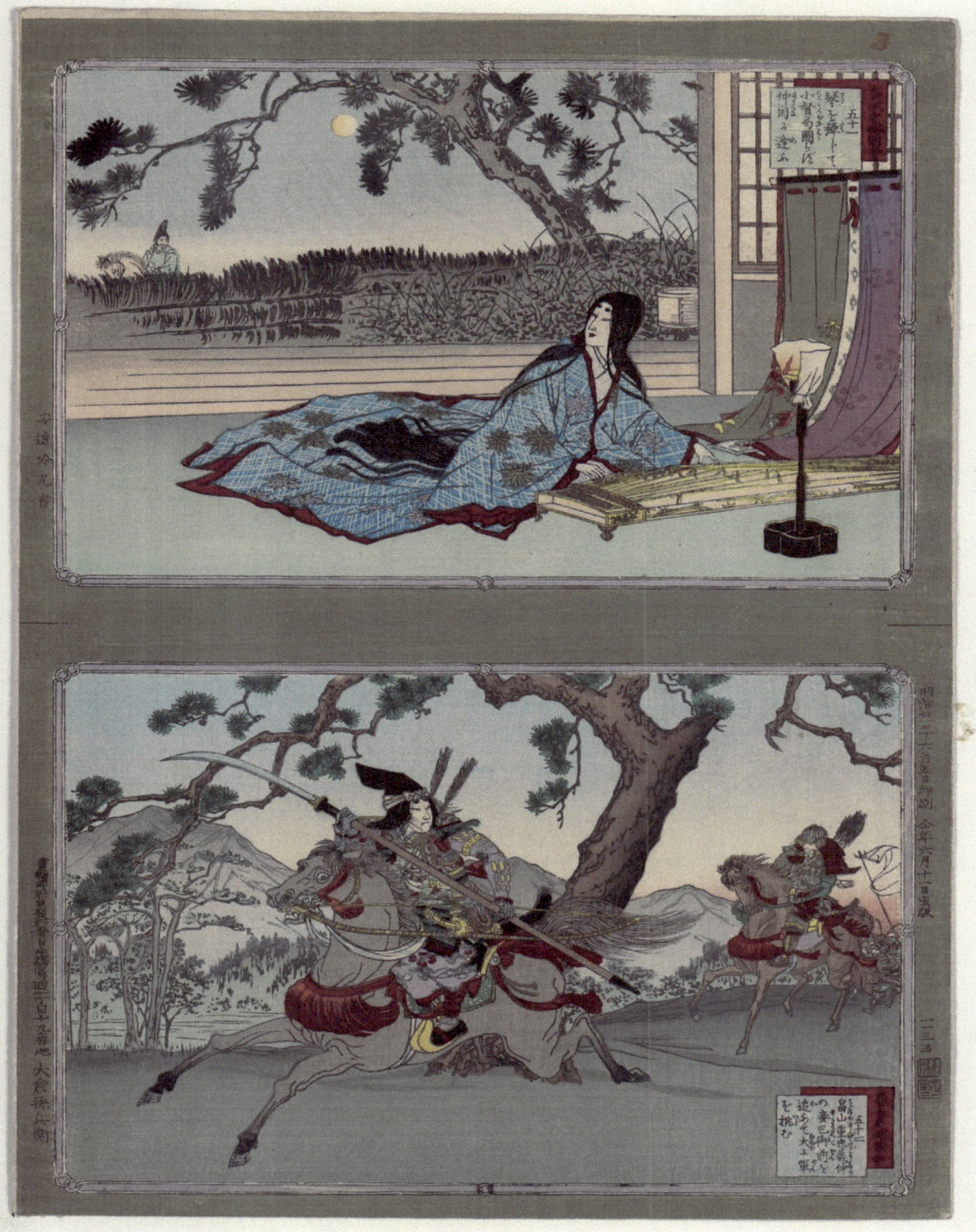

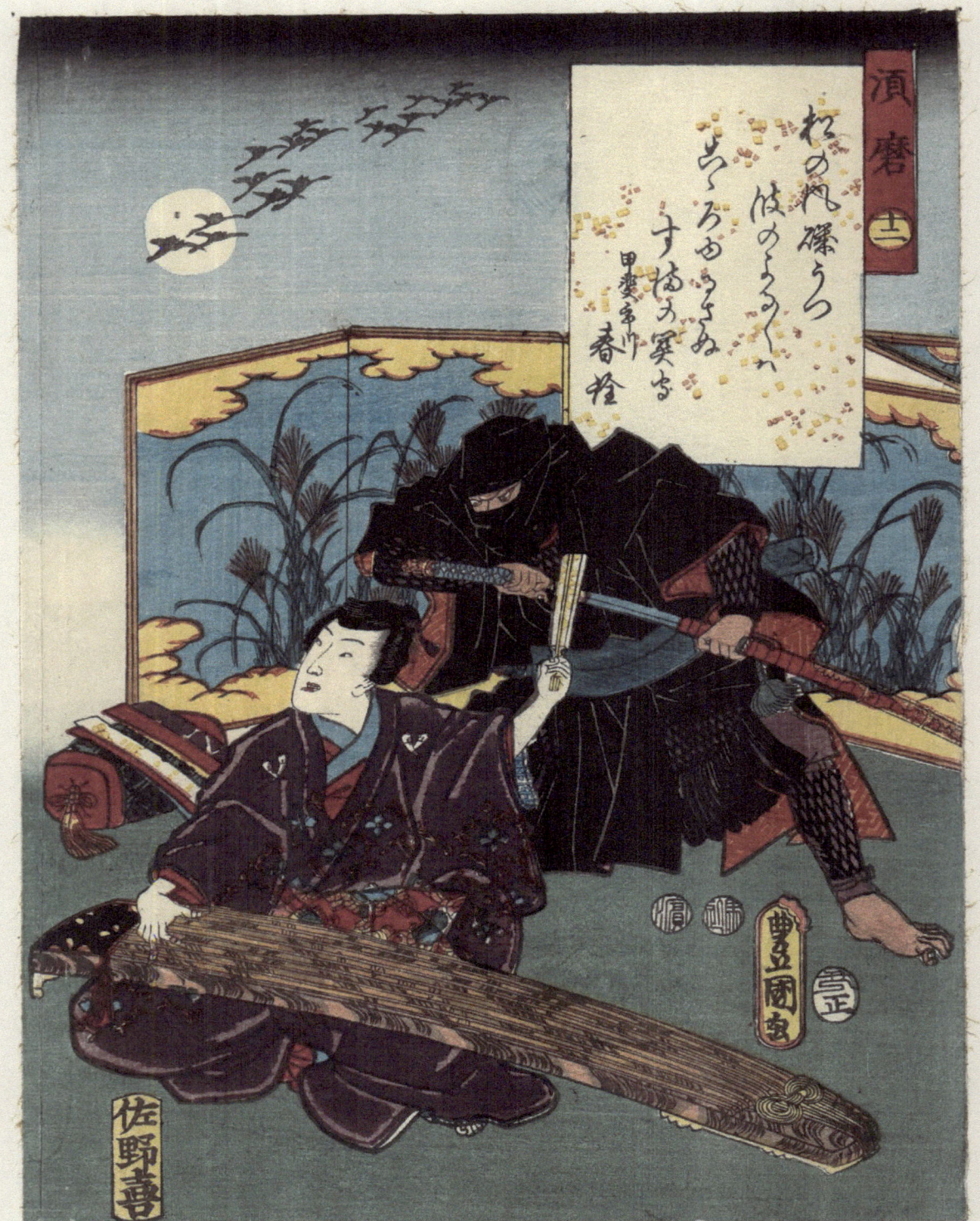

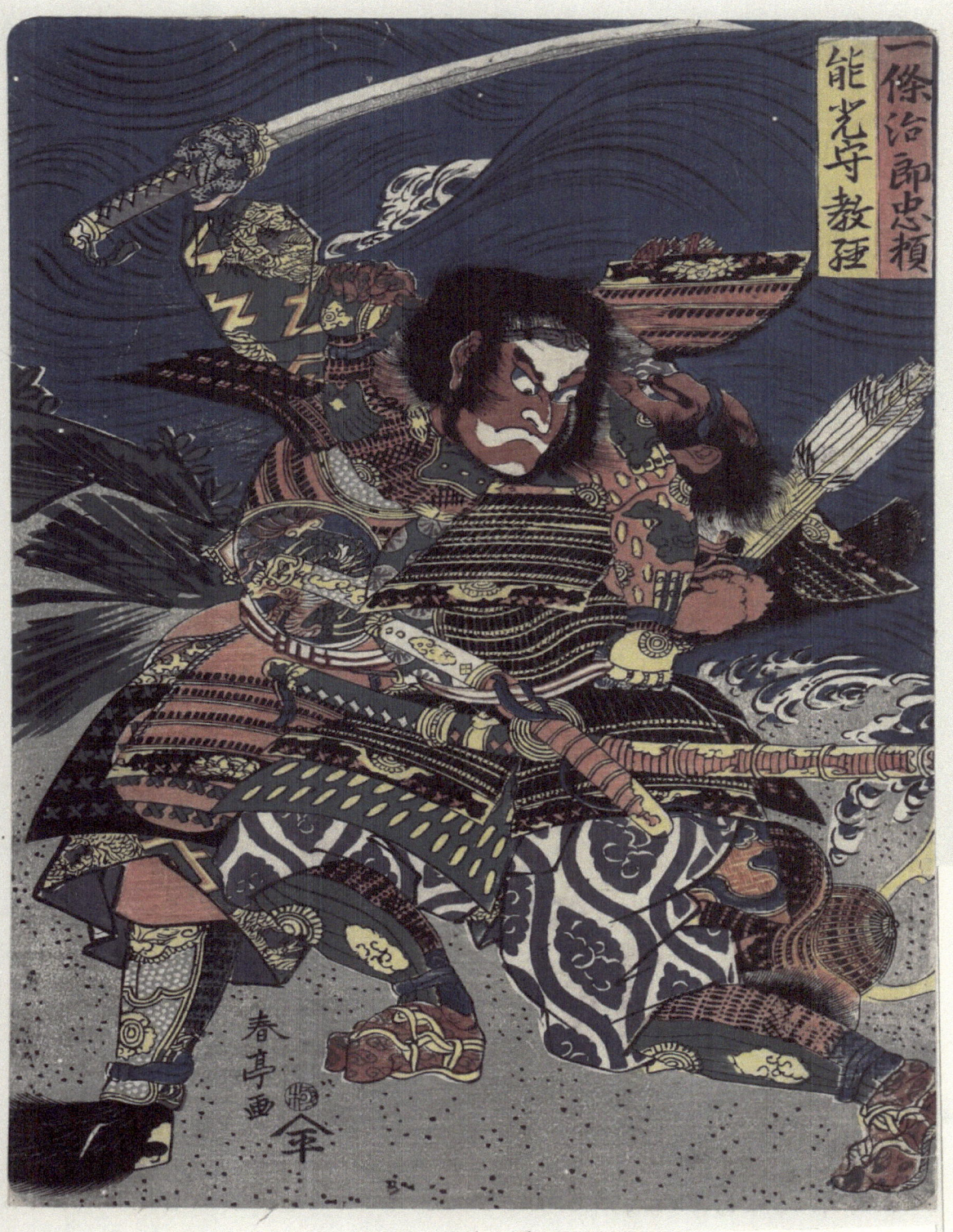

一條冶郎忠頼
能光守 教種

春亭画

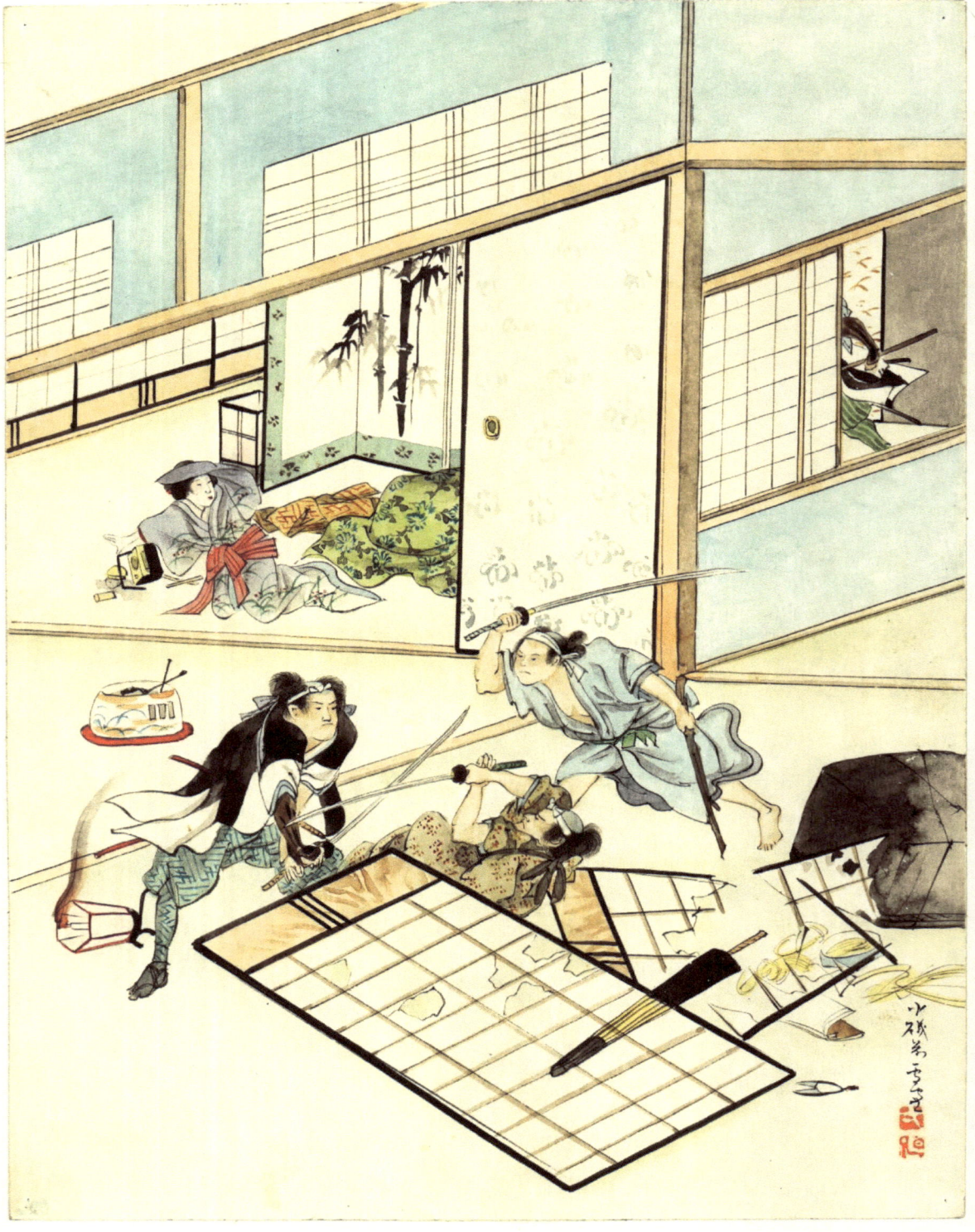

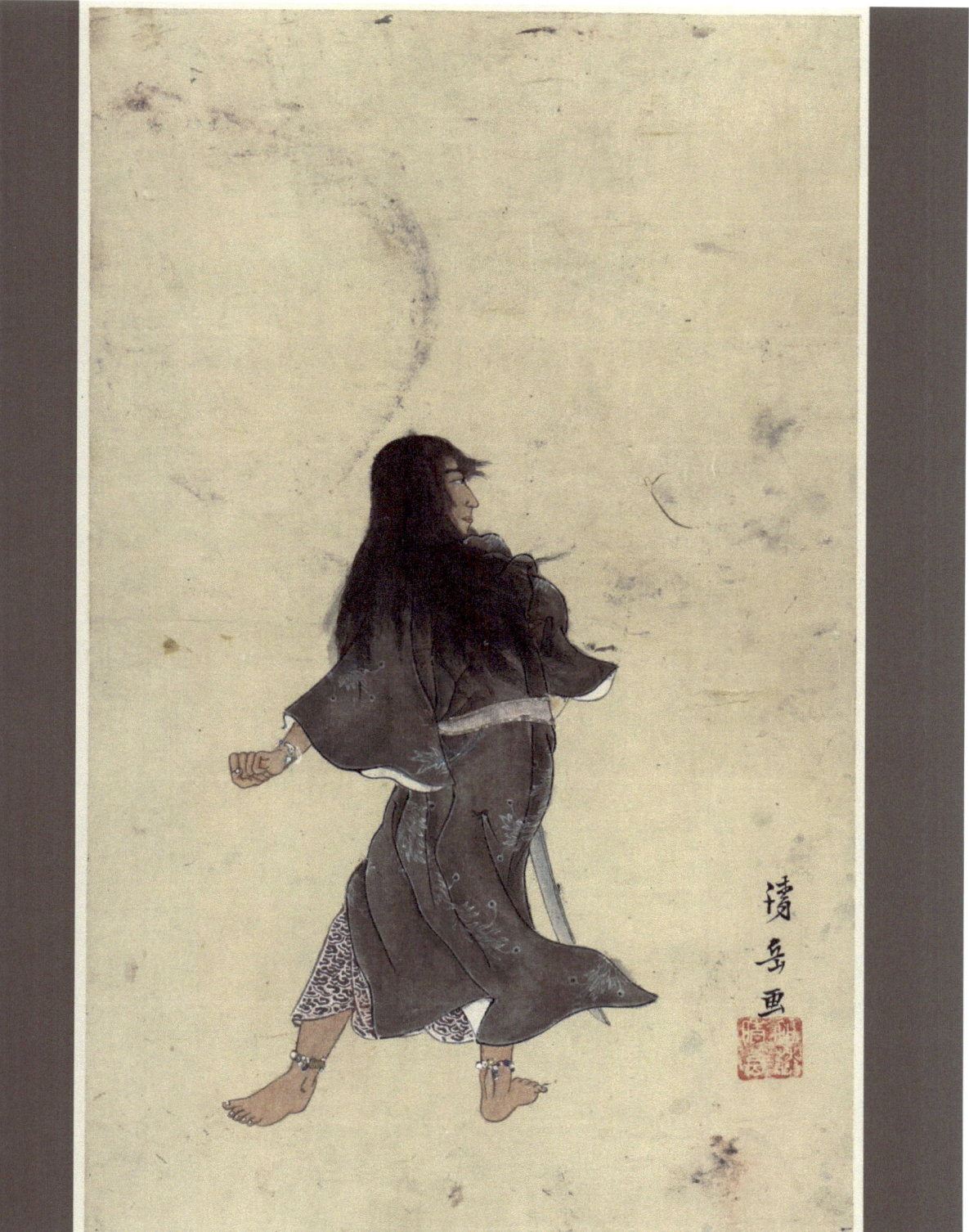

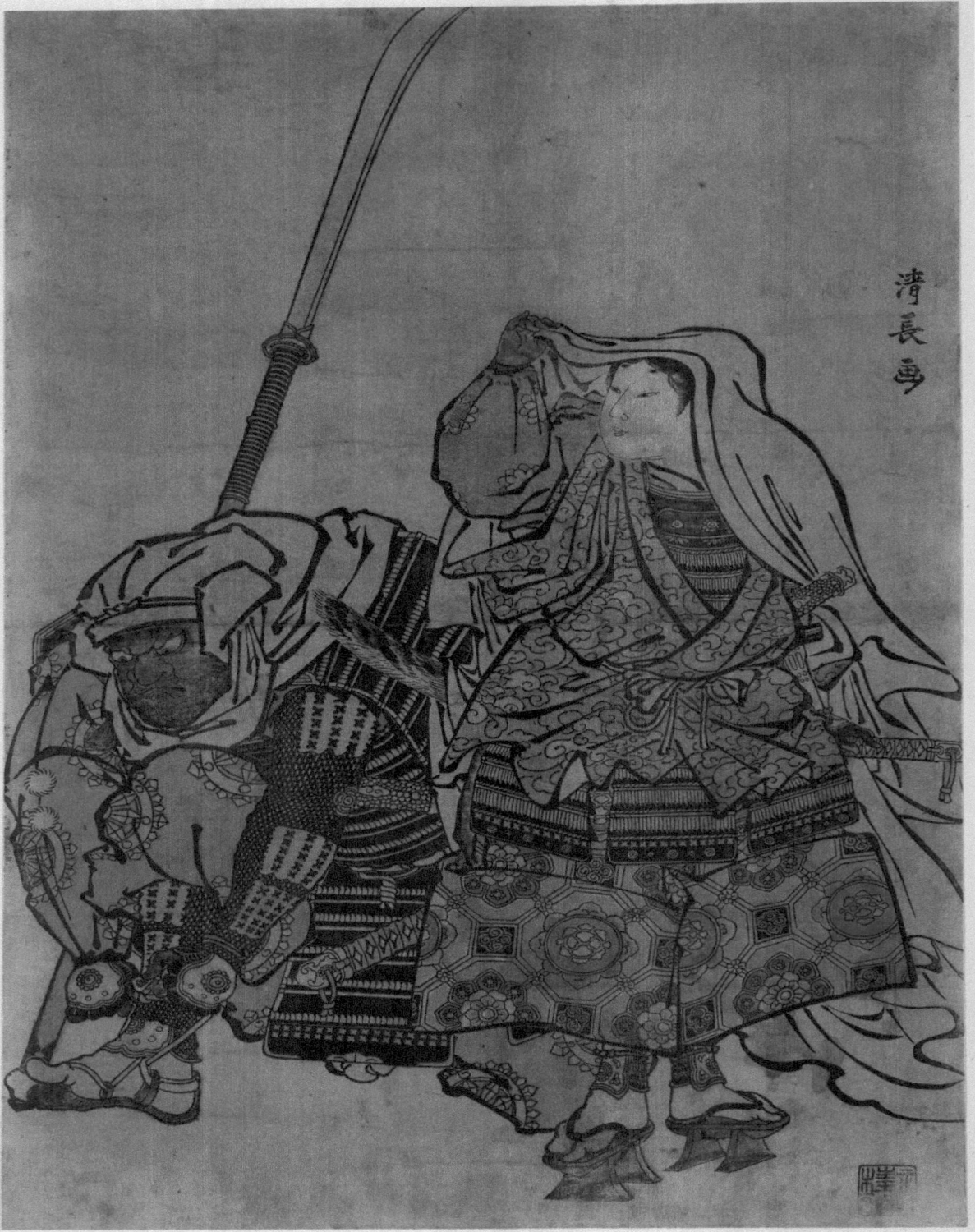

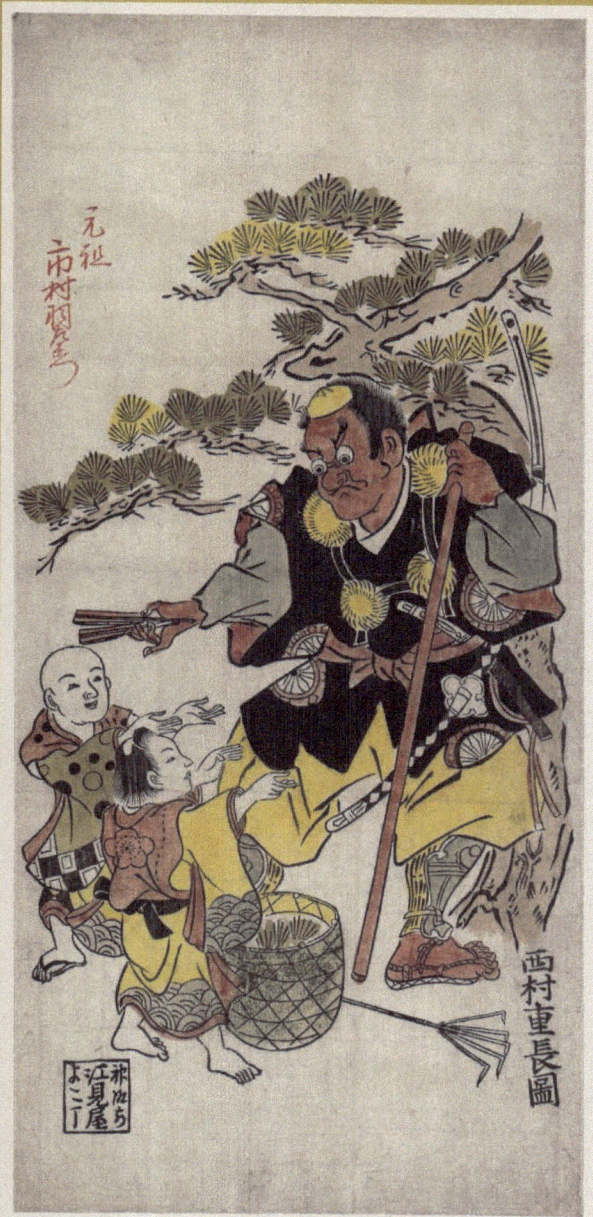

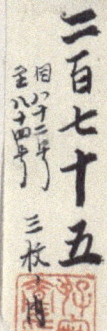

第八十四號　西村重長筆　漆細絵一枚

二百七十五
三枚

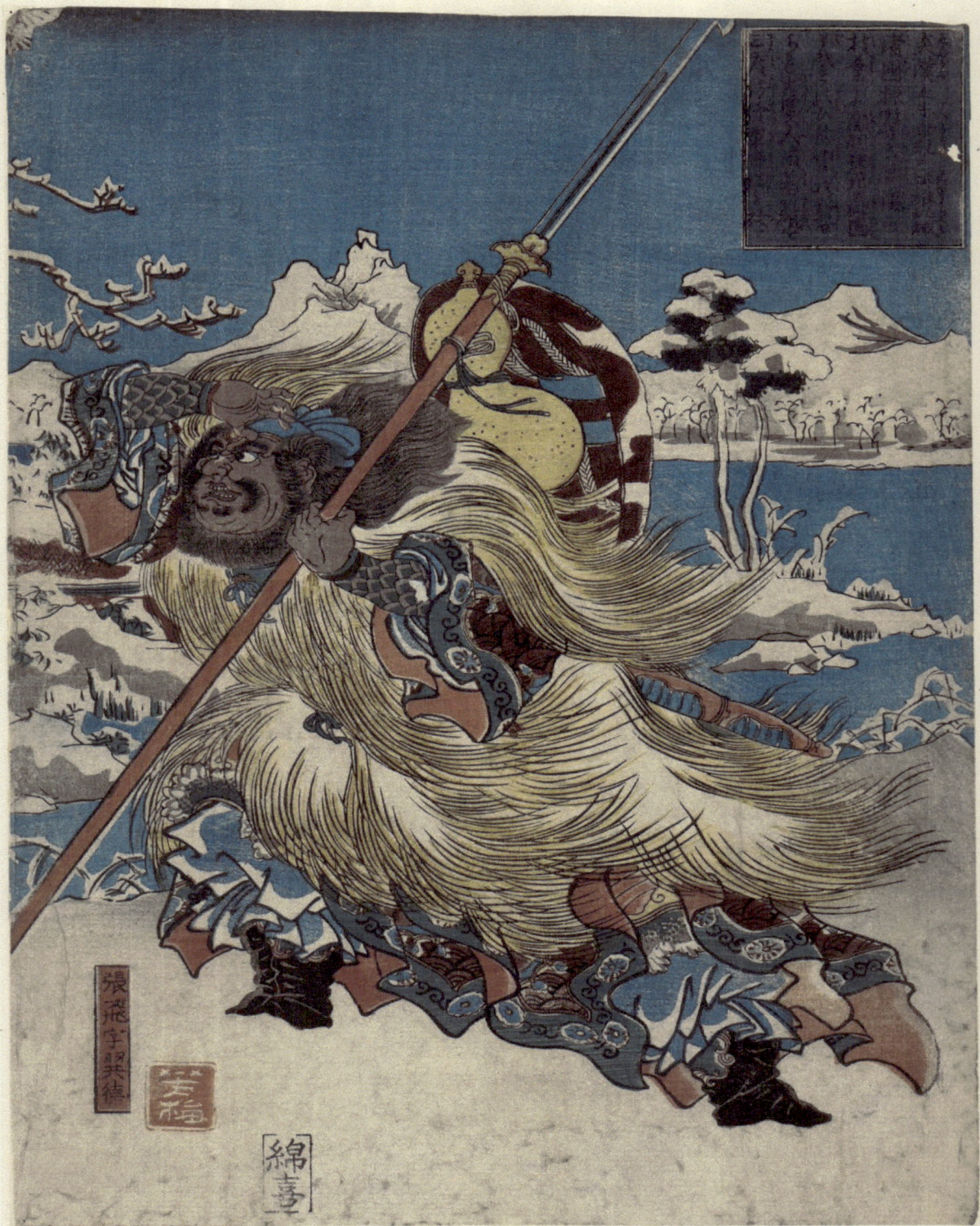

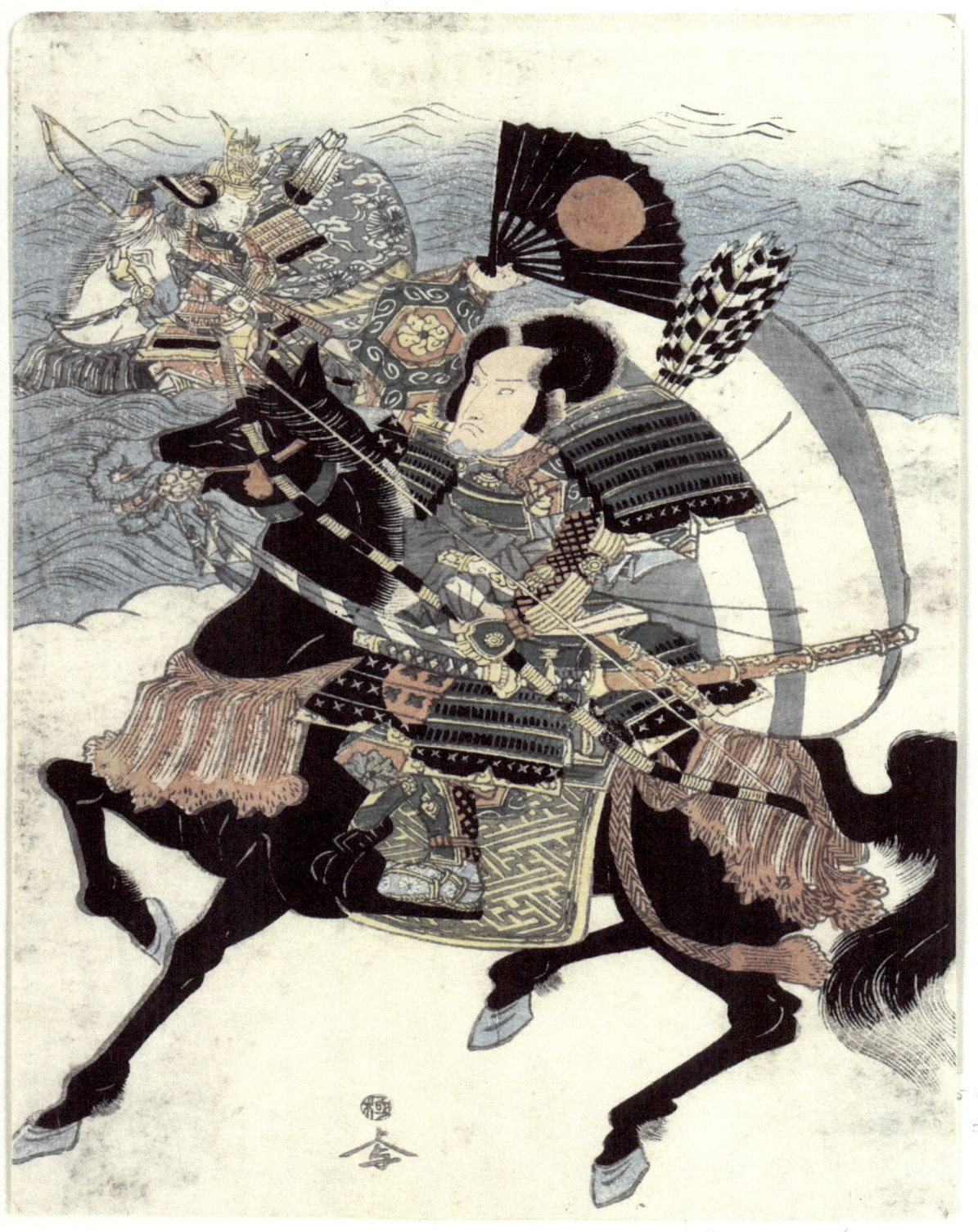

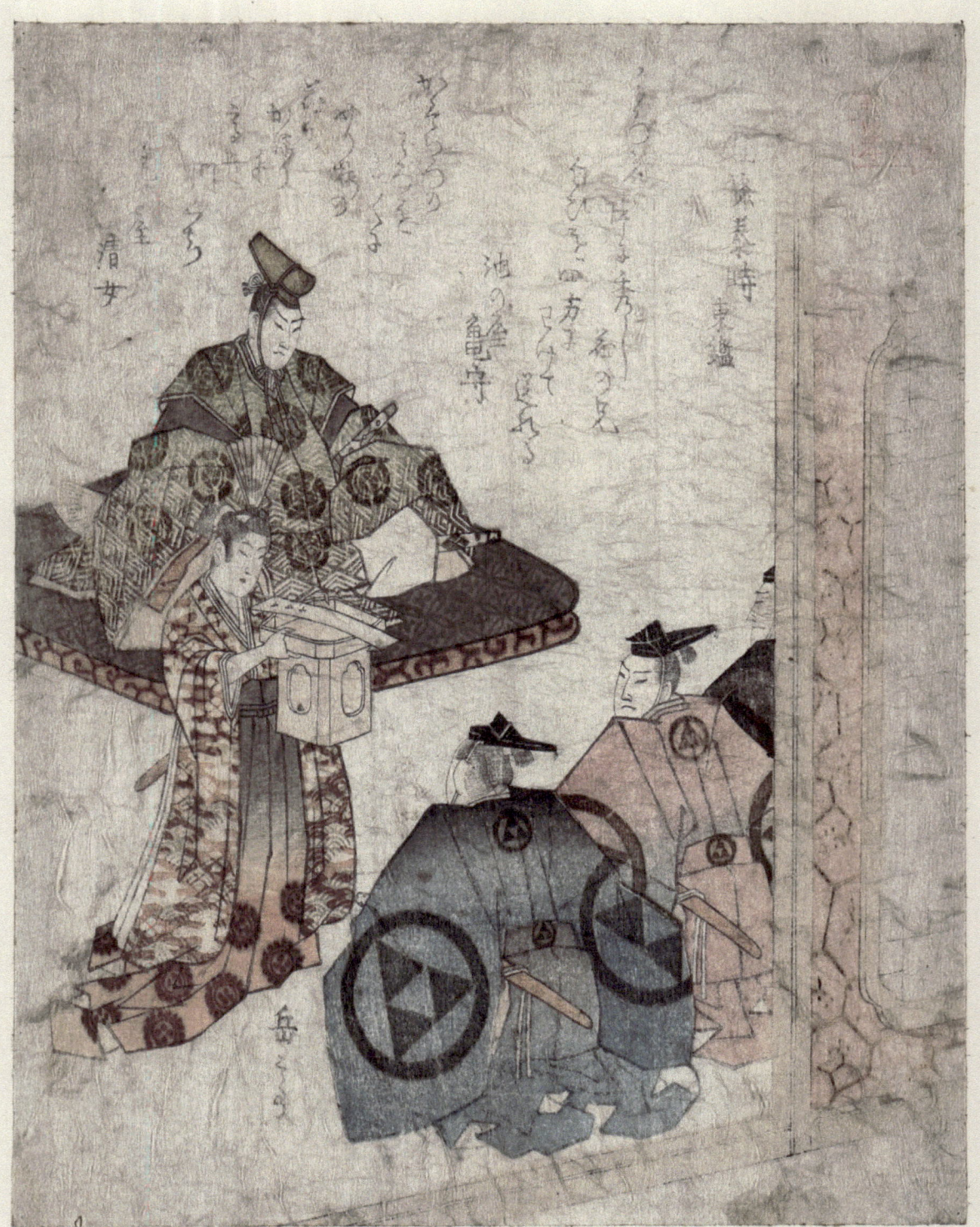

御随身

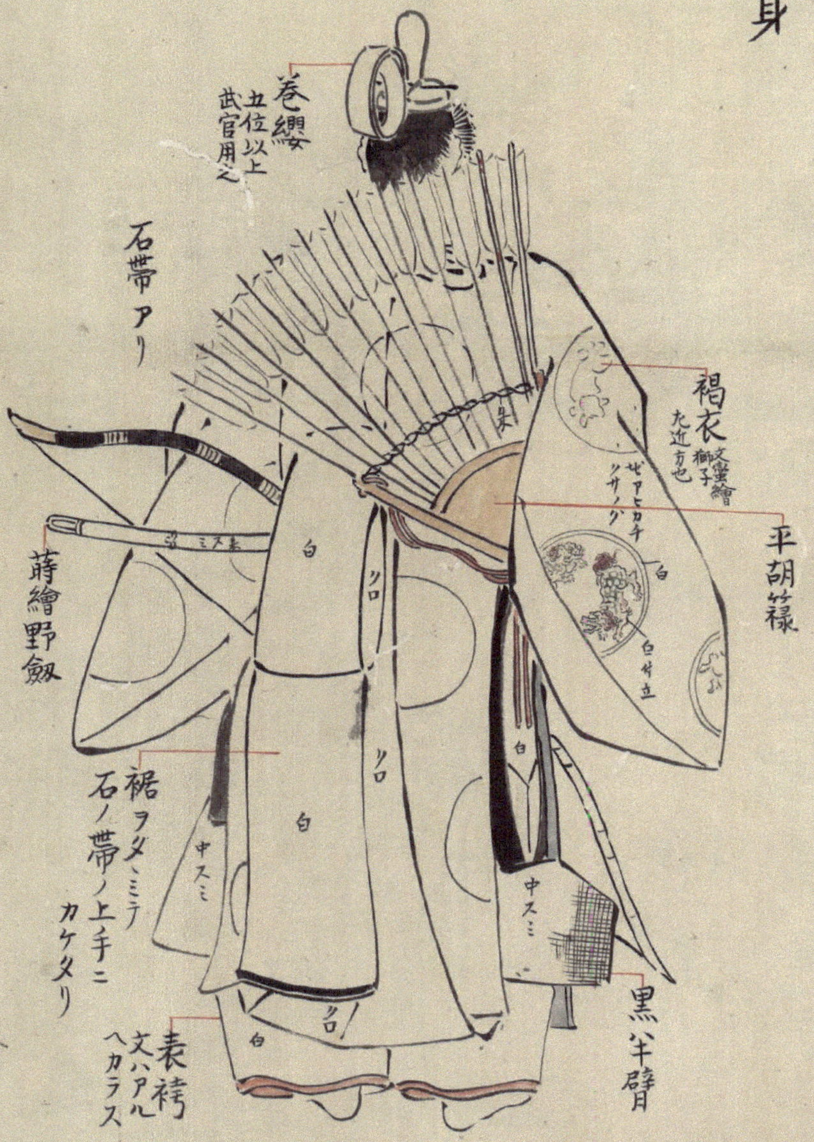

巻纓
五位以上
武官用之

石帯アリ

褐衣
文蛮繪
獅子
左近方也

平胡簶

ゼアヒカチ
クサゝク

白

白

白
白

蒔繪
野劔

クロ

クロ

白

白

中スミ

白

中スミ

裾
ヲダミニテ
石ノ帯ノ上手ニ
カケタリ

黒半臂

白

表袴
文ハアル
ヘカラス

十

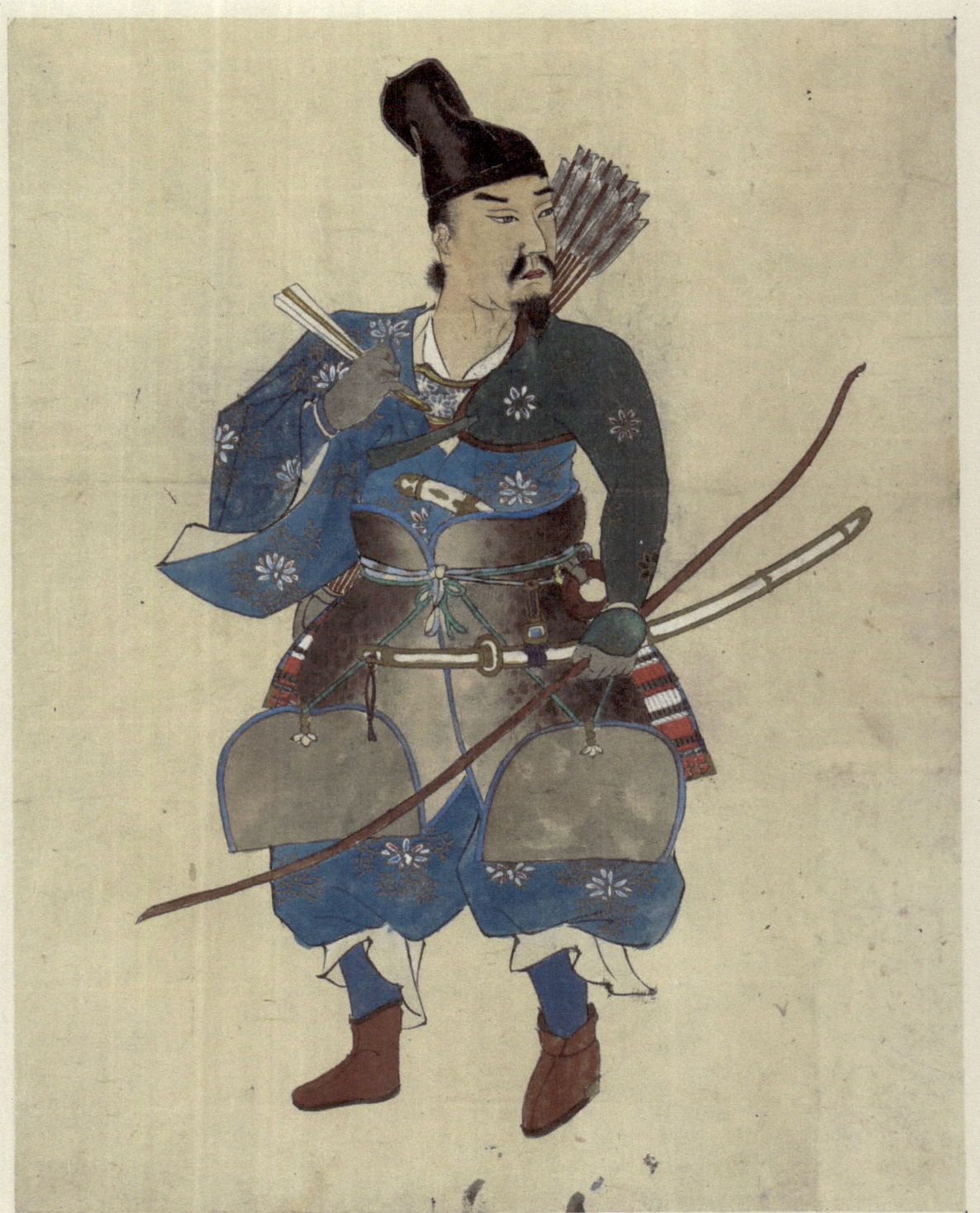

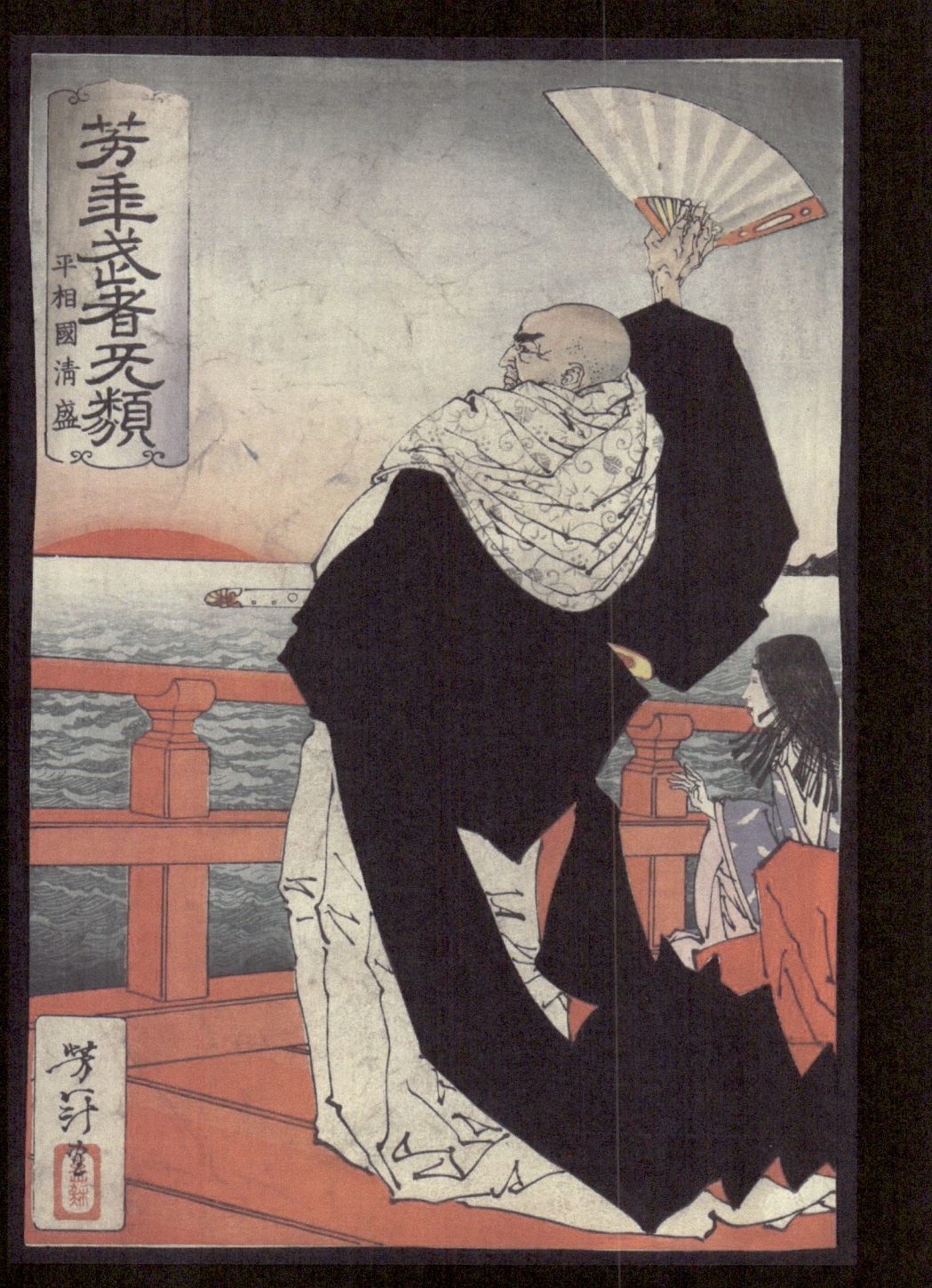

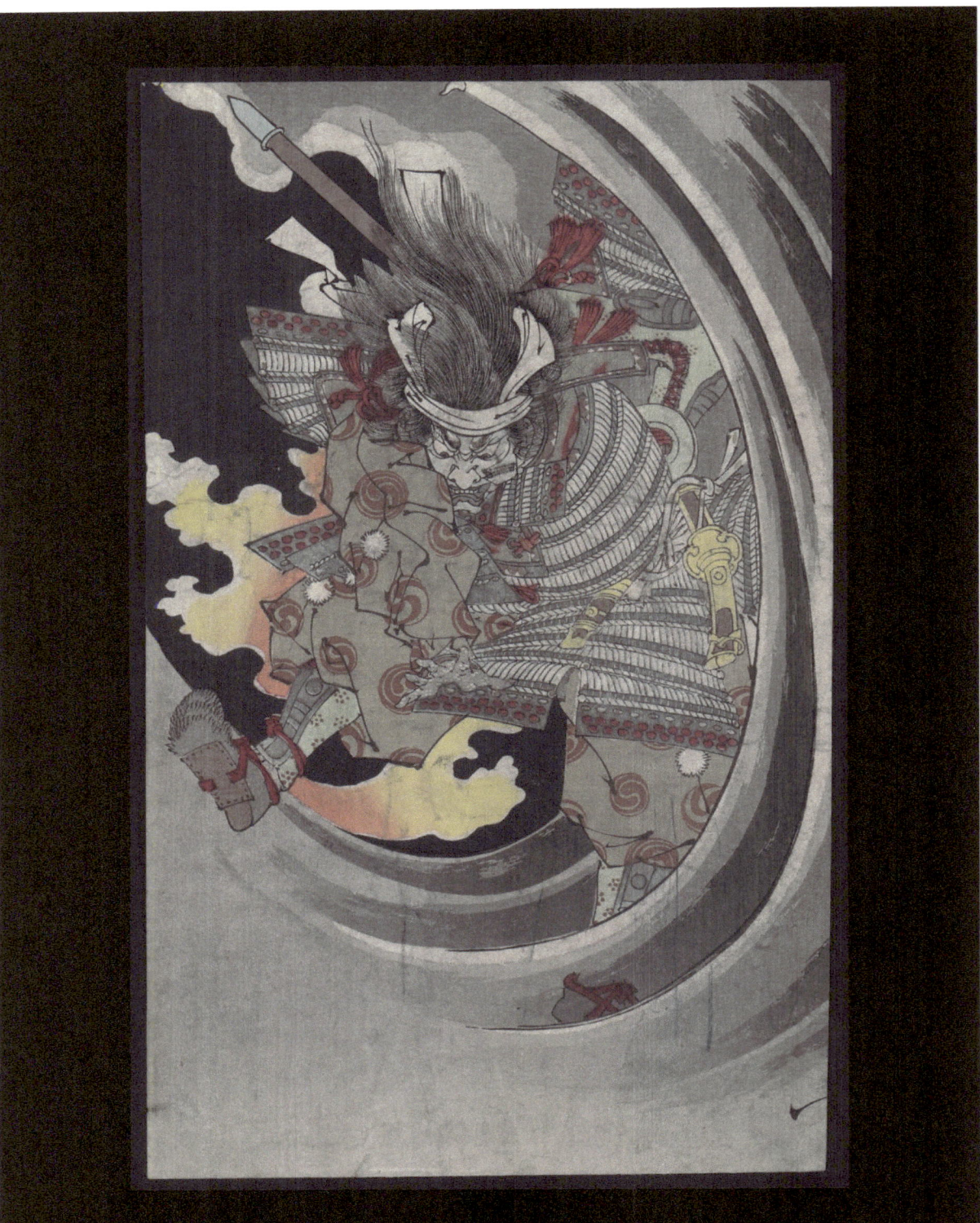

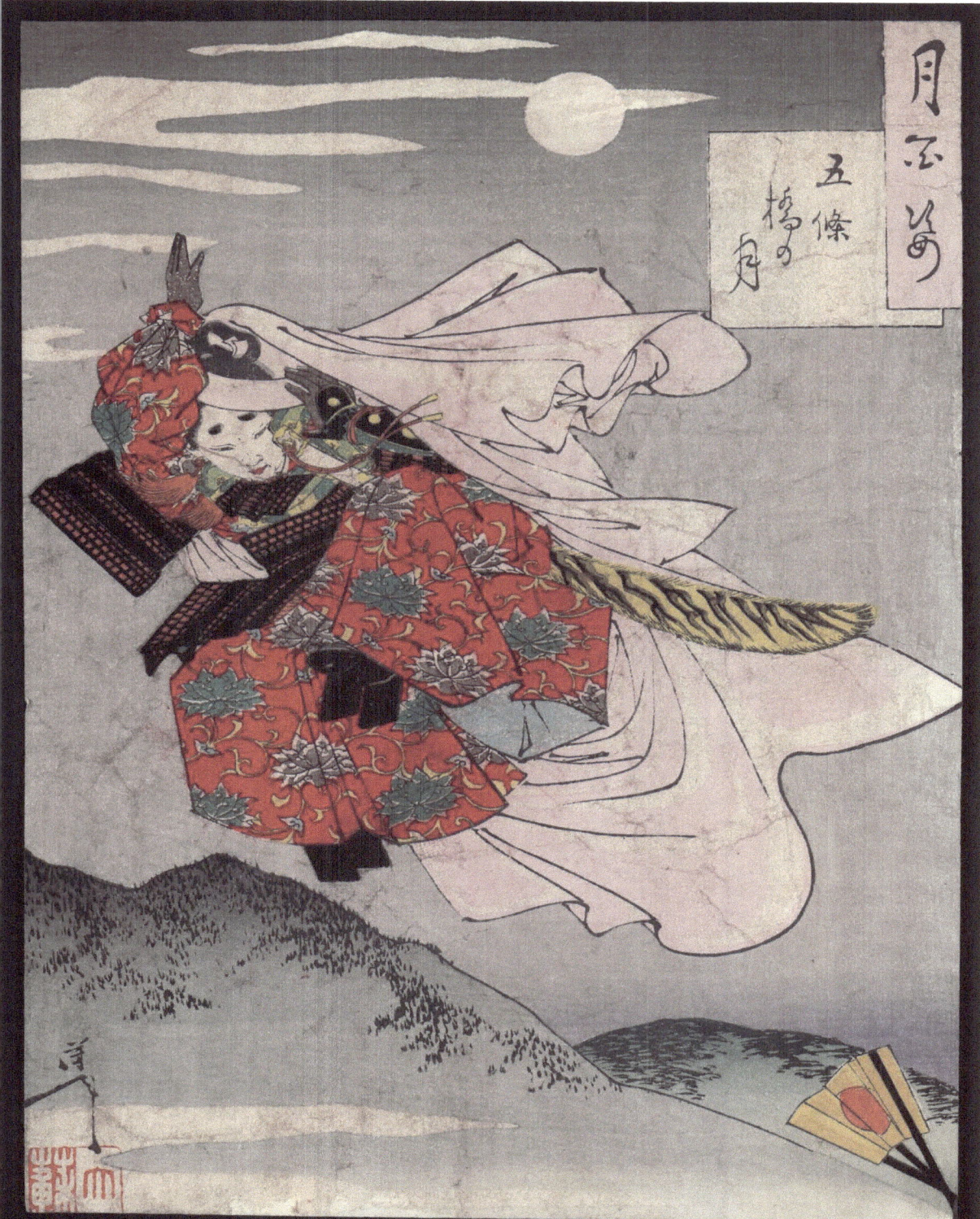

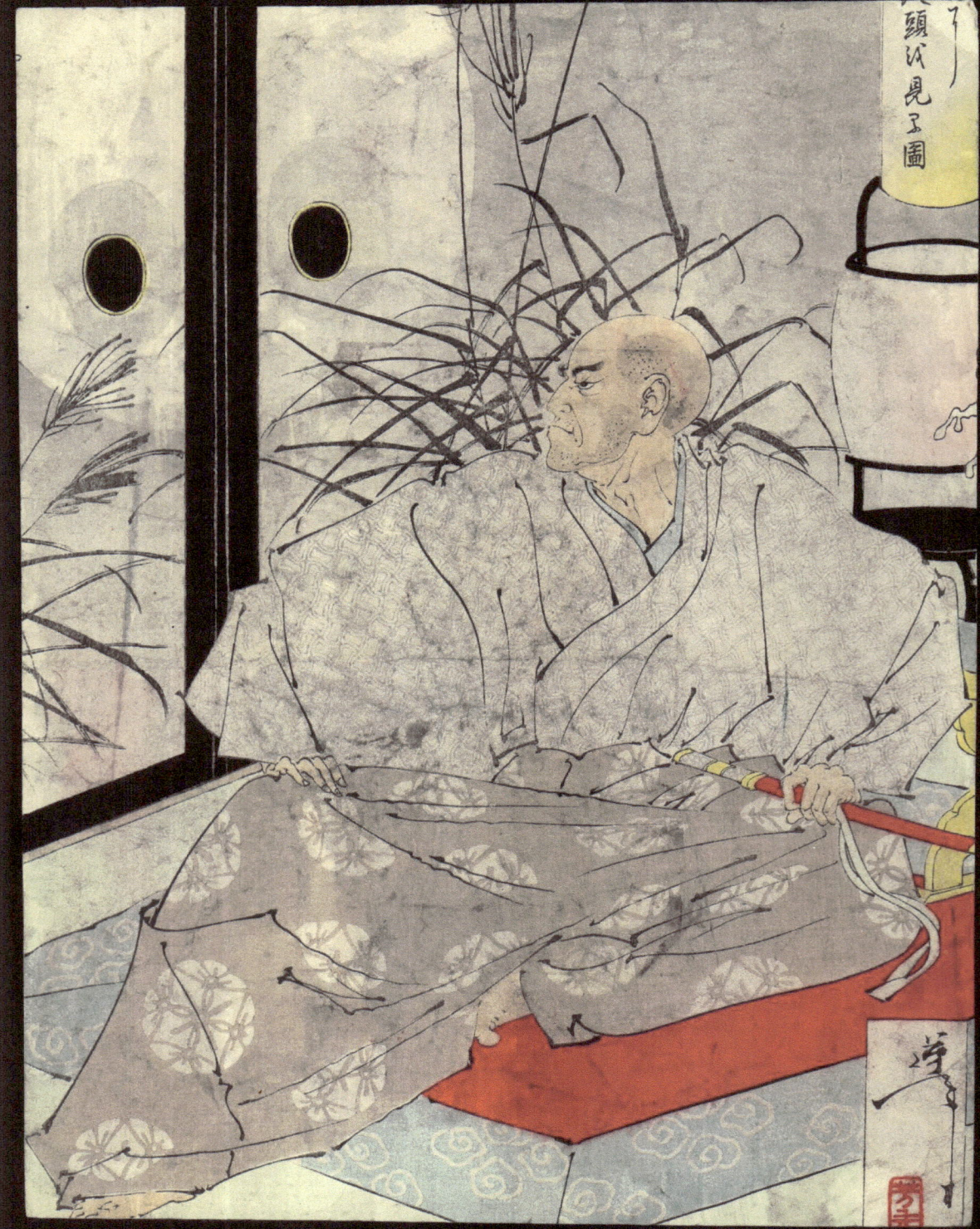

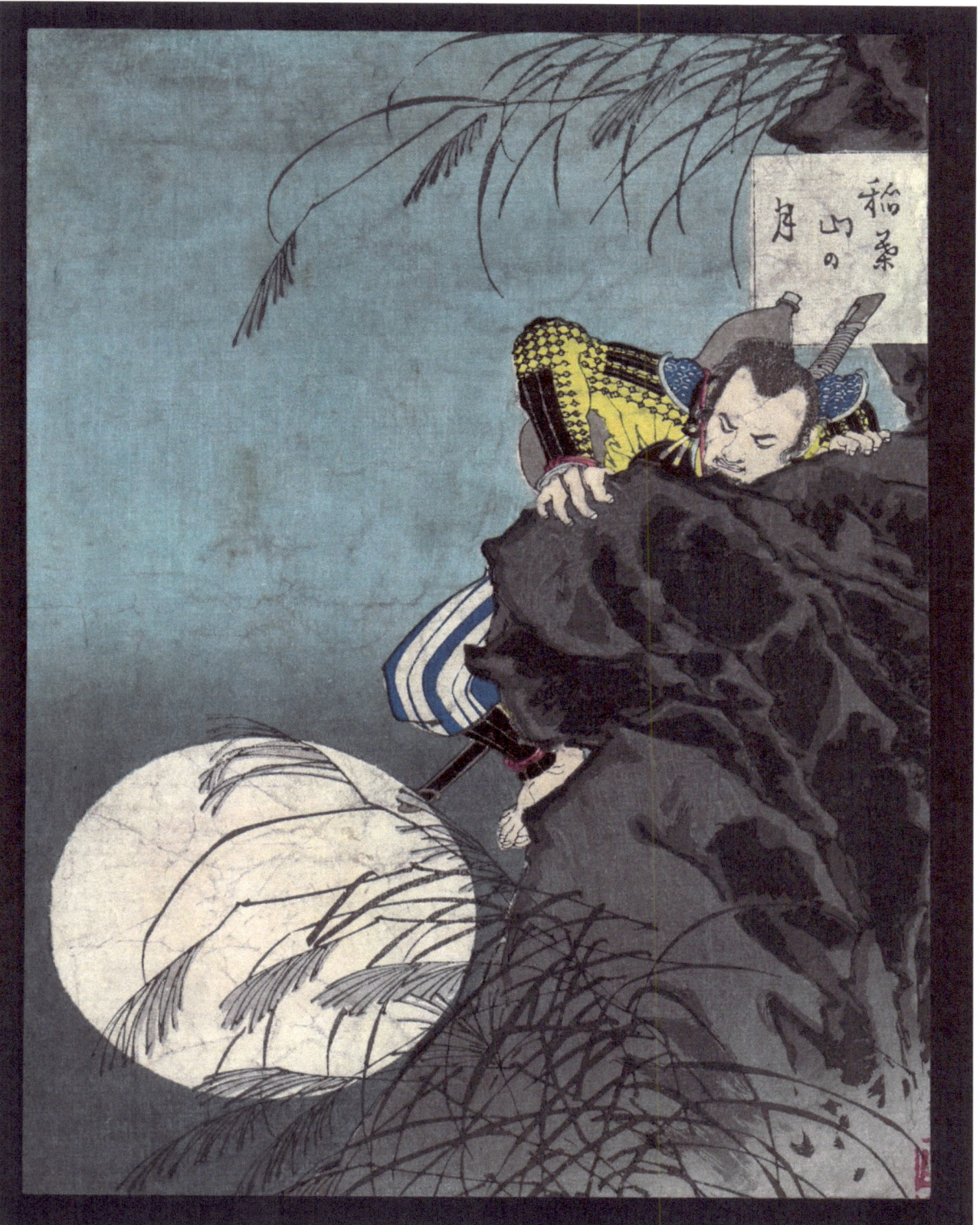

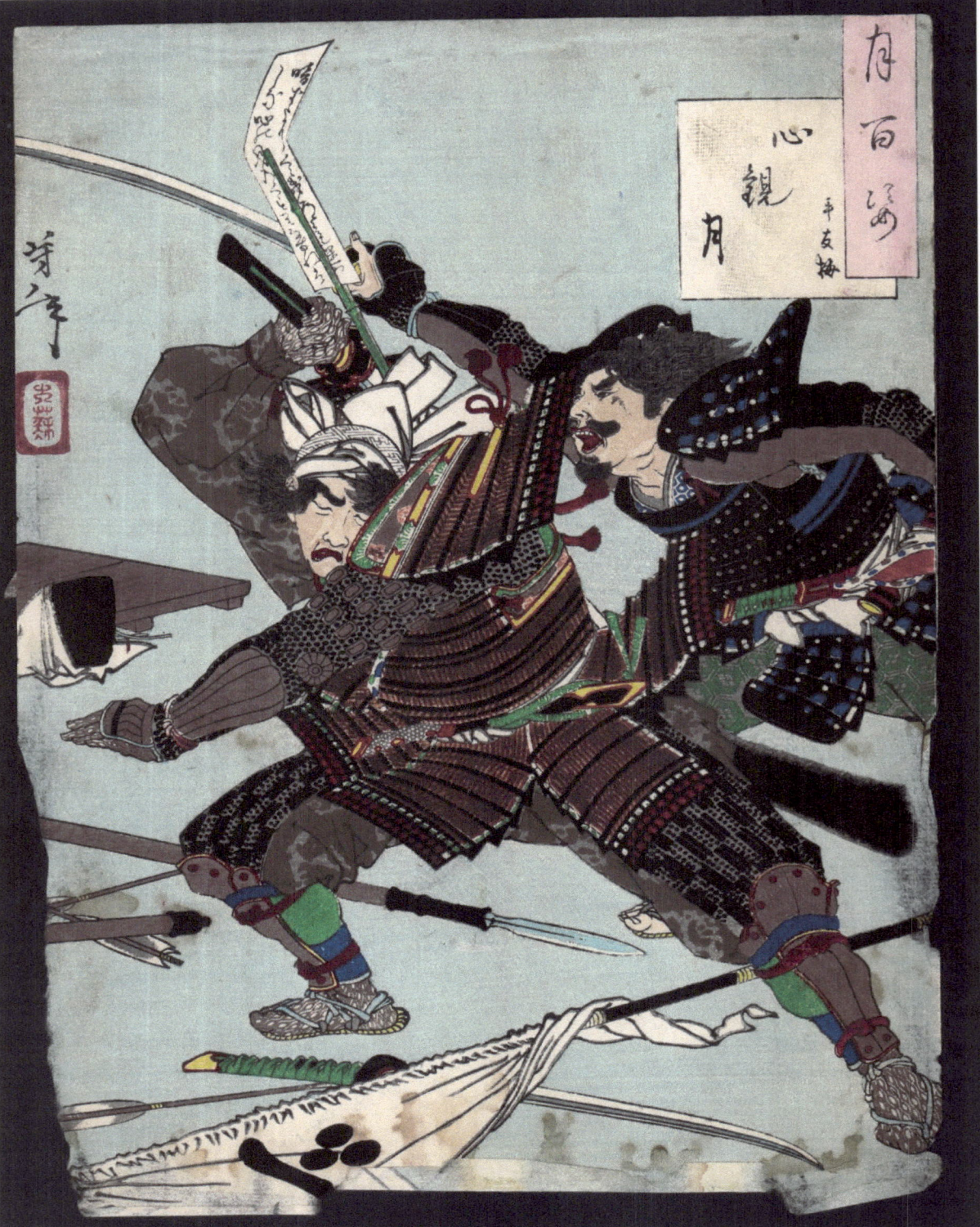

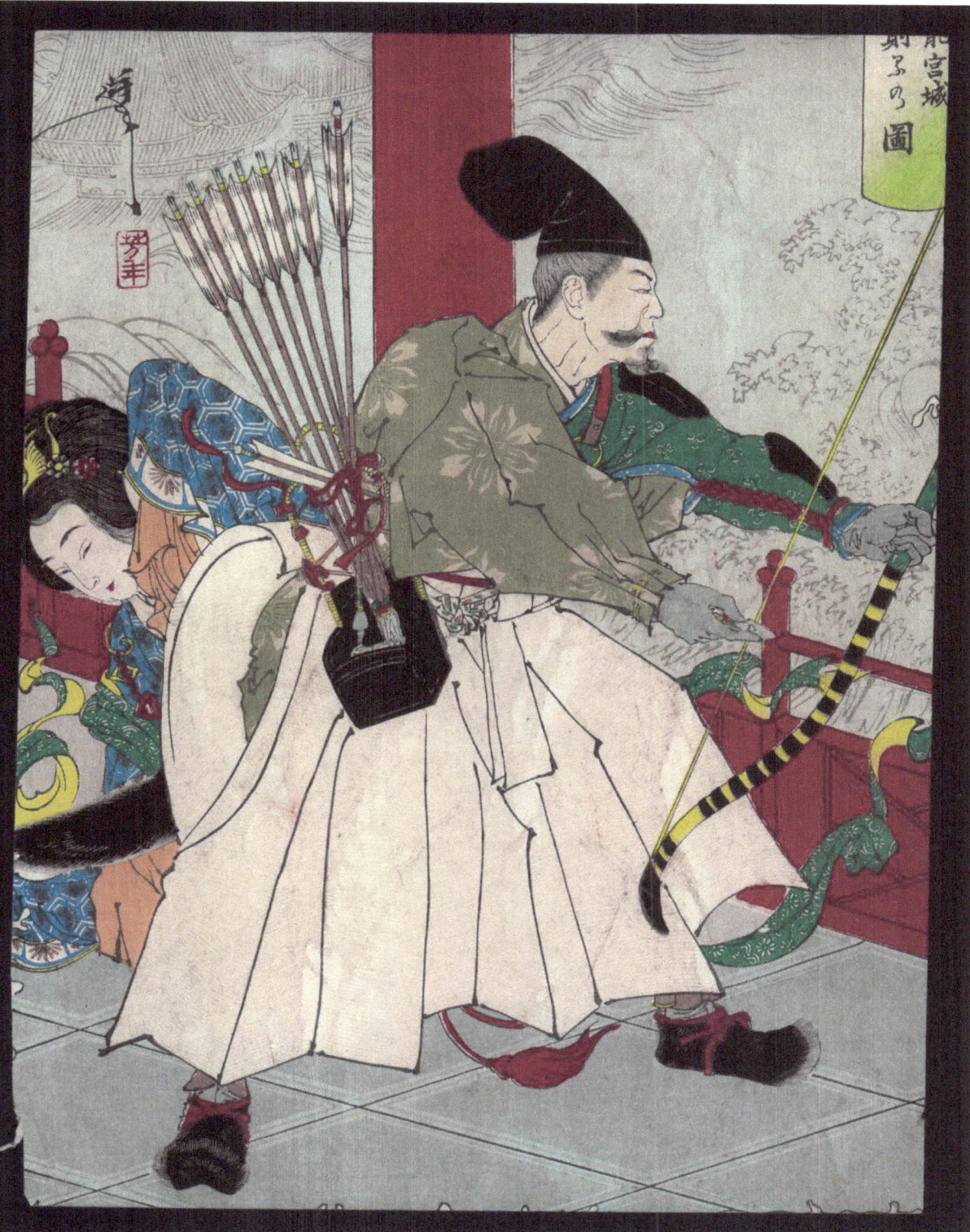

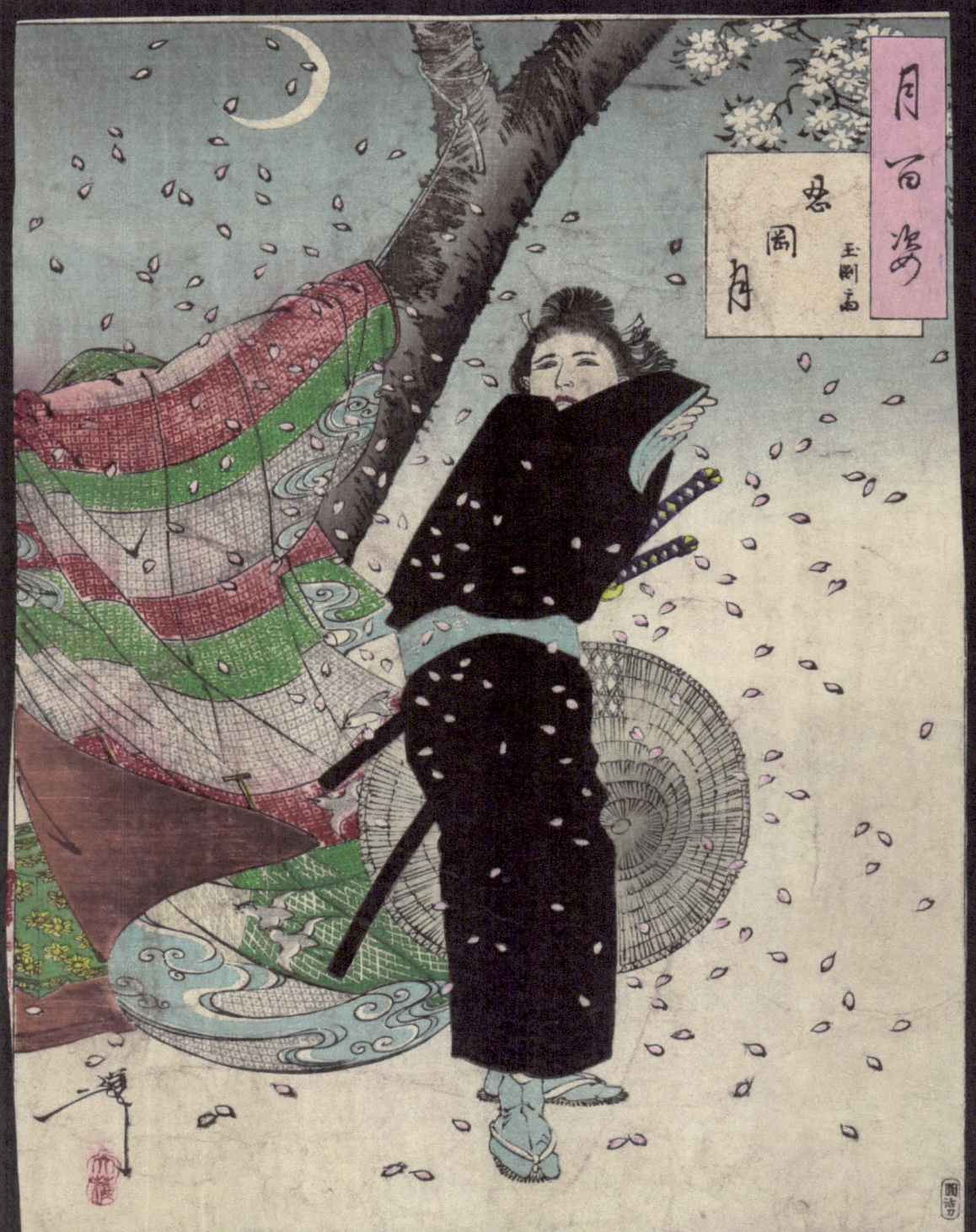

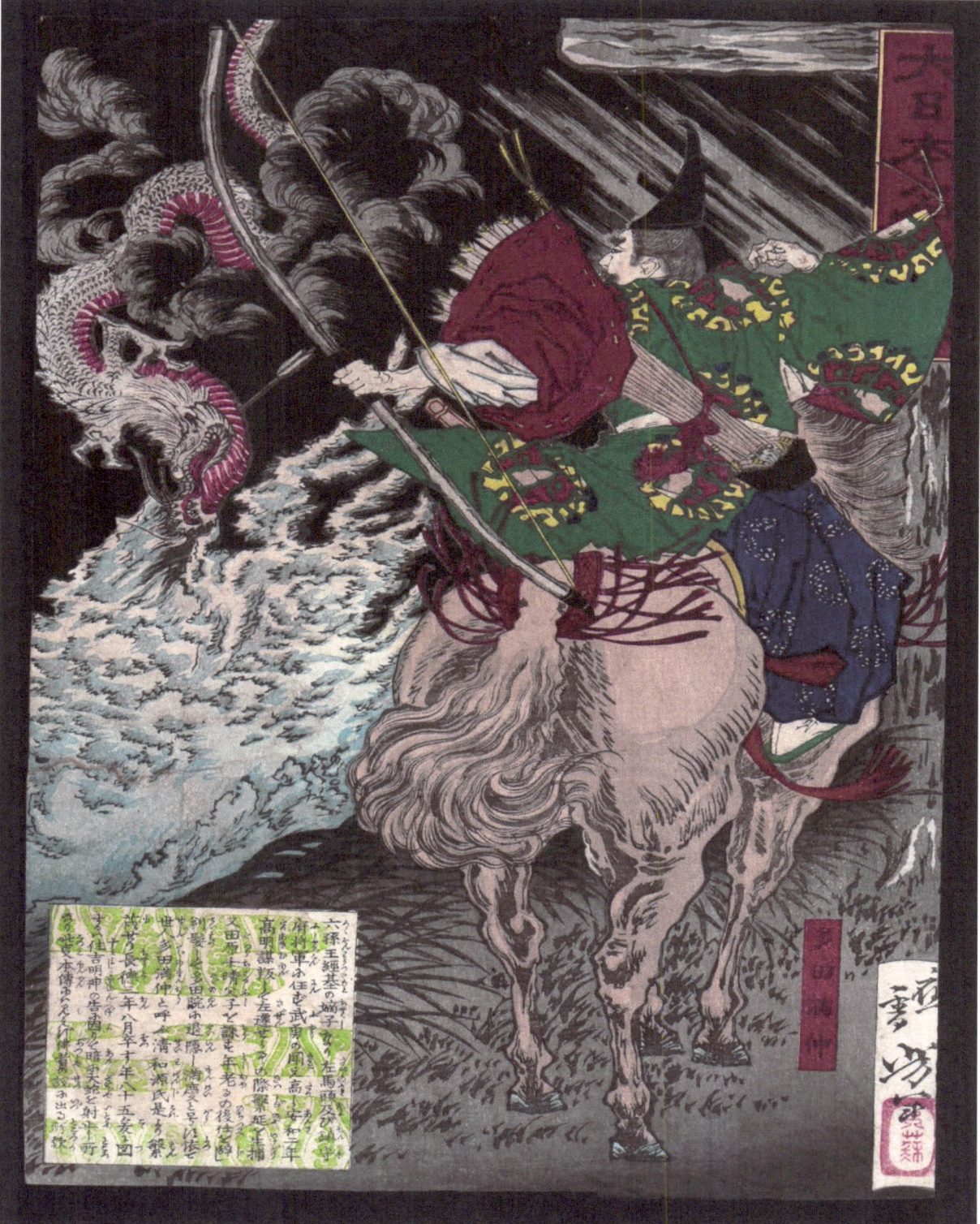

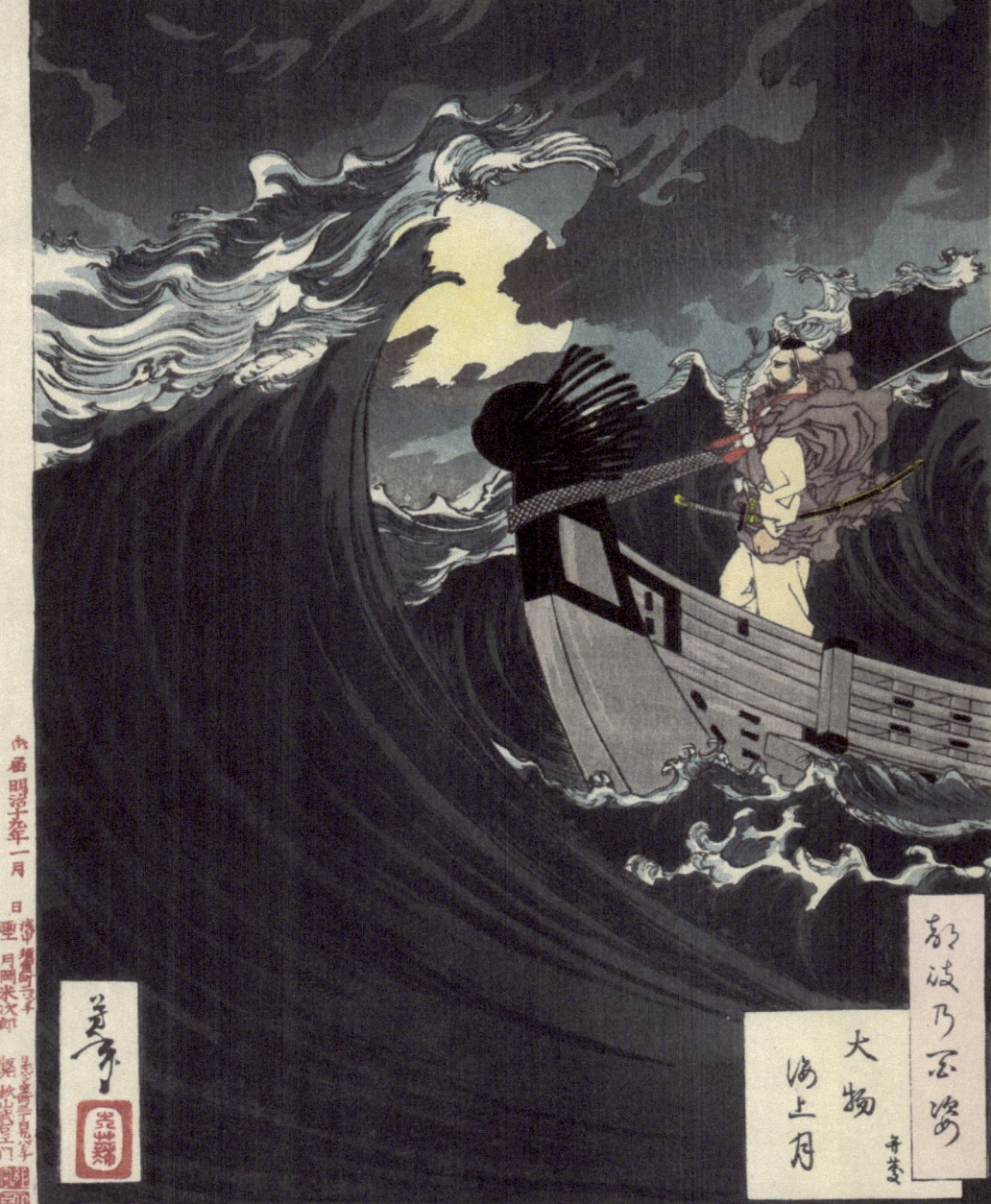

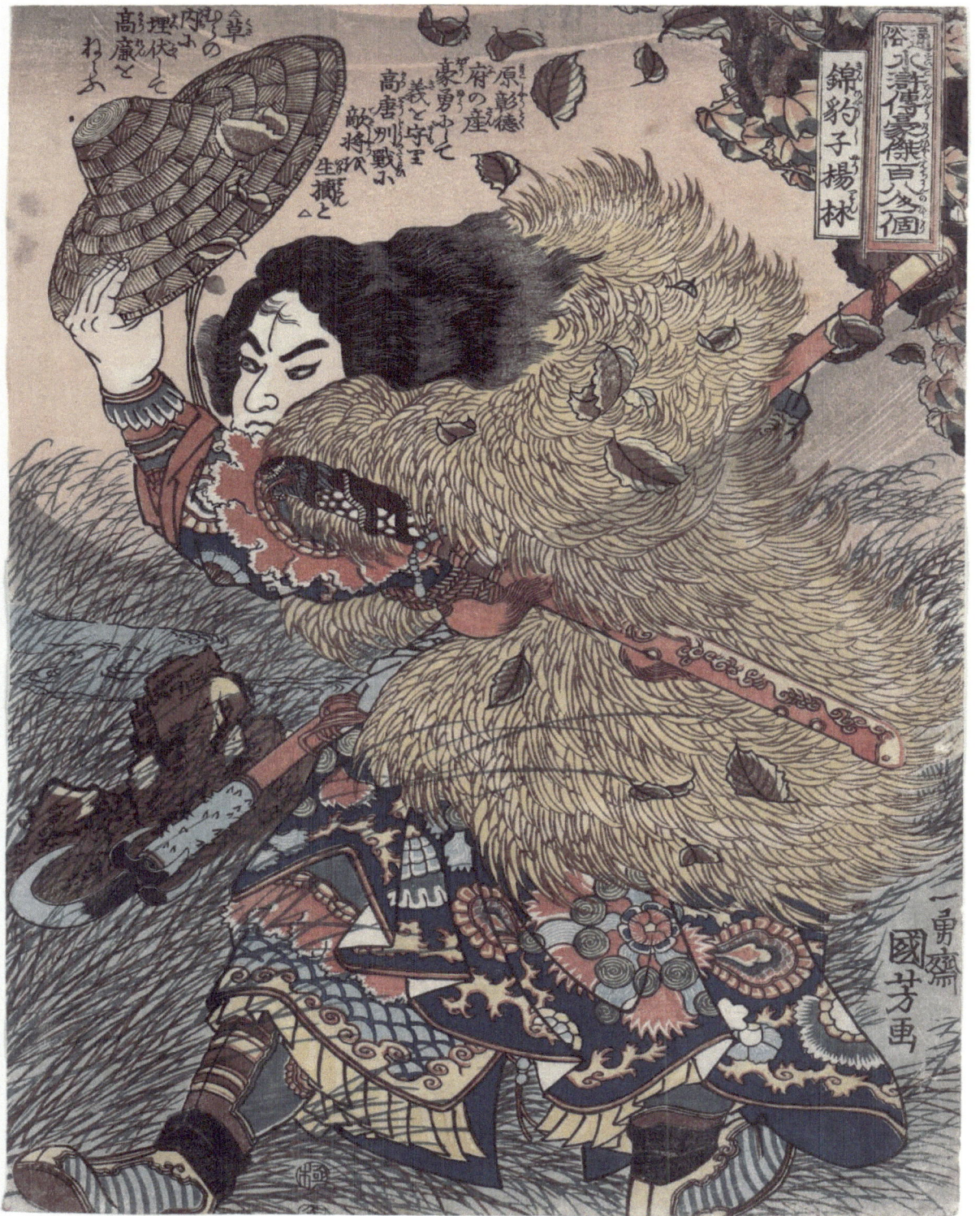

通俗水滸傳豪傑百八個

錦豹子楊林

草野の内に埋伏して高廉をねらふ

原彰德府の産
豪勇ゆ／て義を守り
高唐州の戰ひ
敵將を生擒と

一勇齋
國芳画

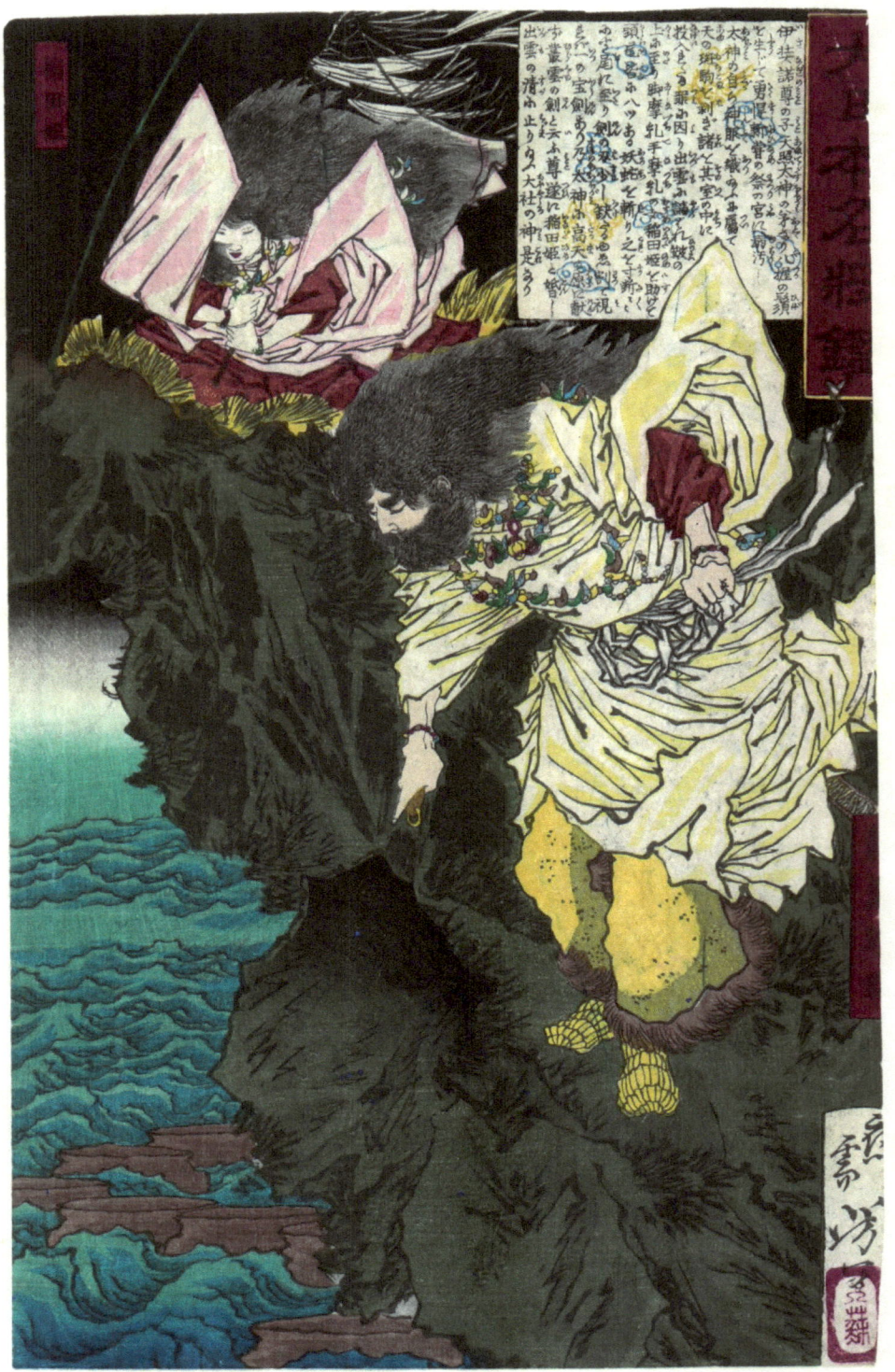

芳年

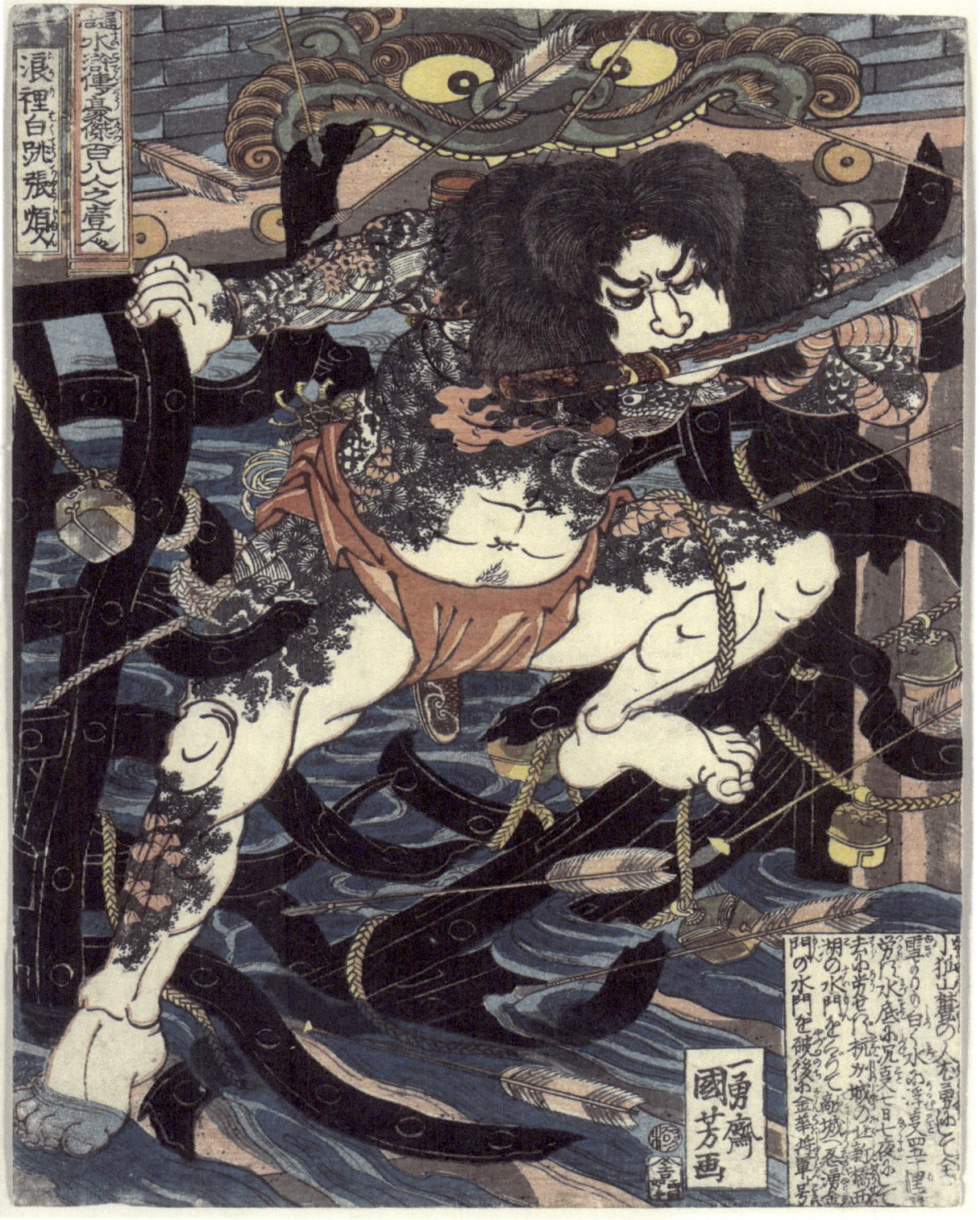

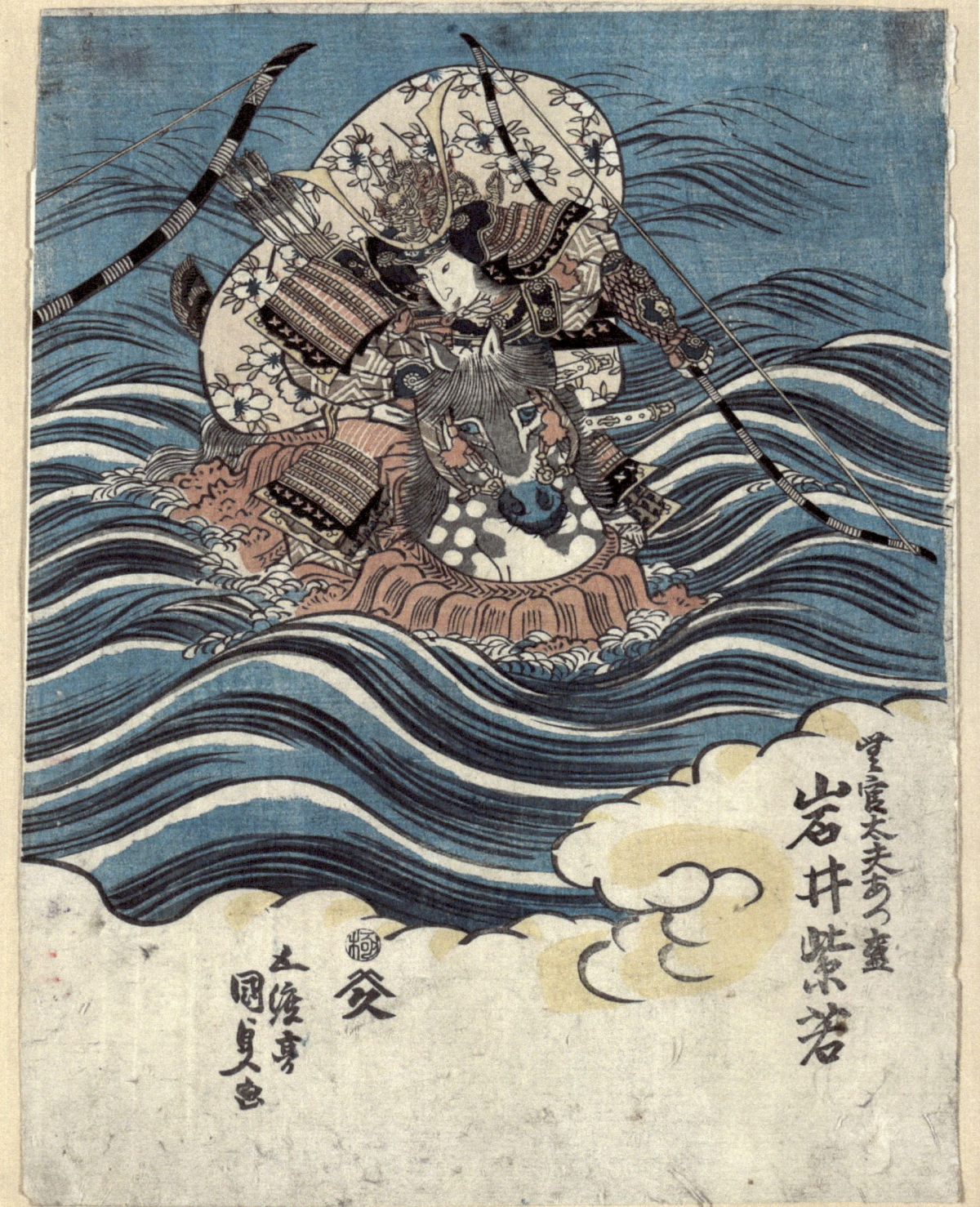

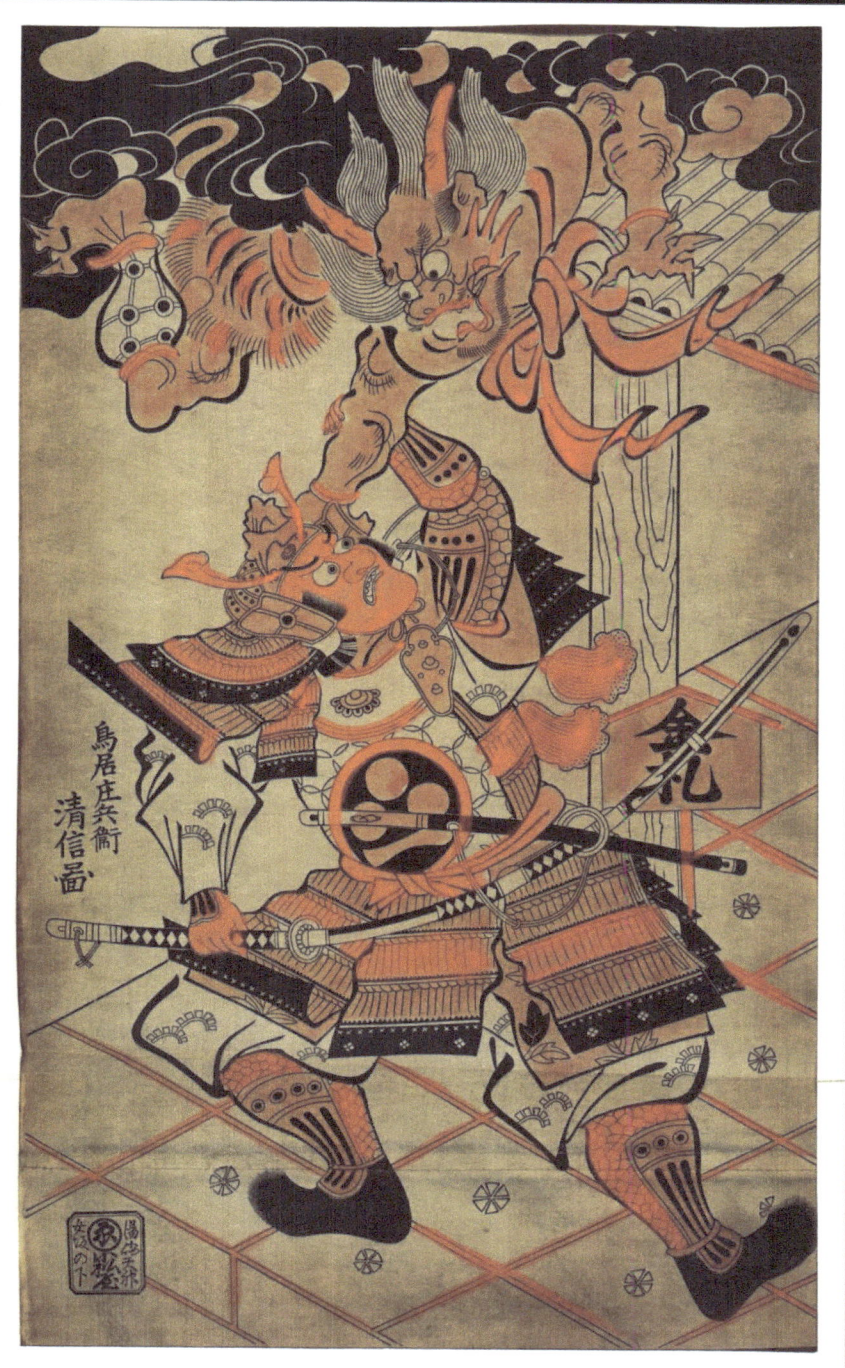

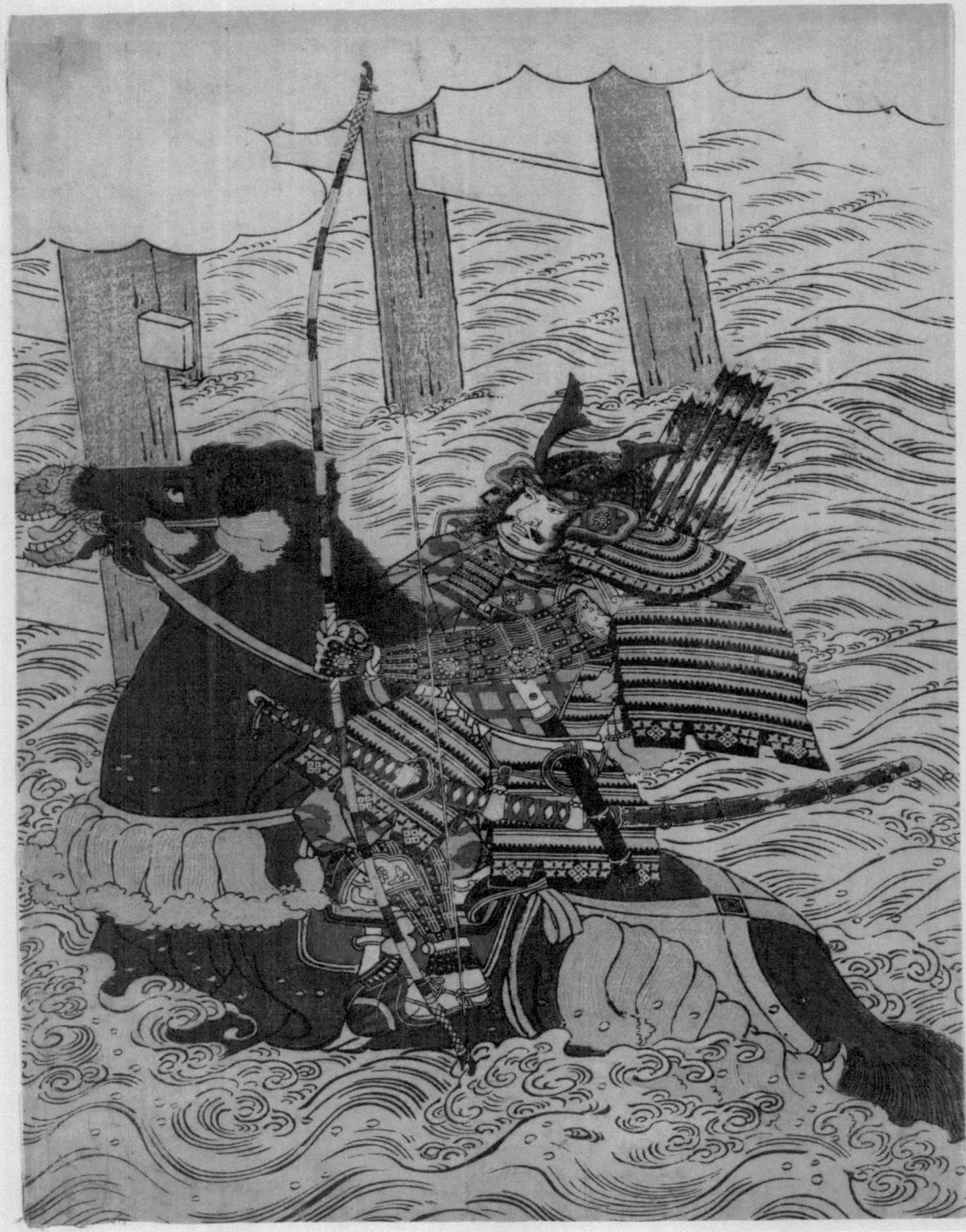

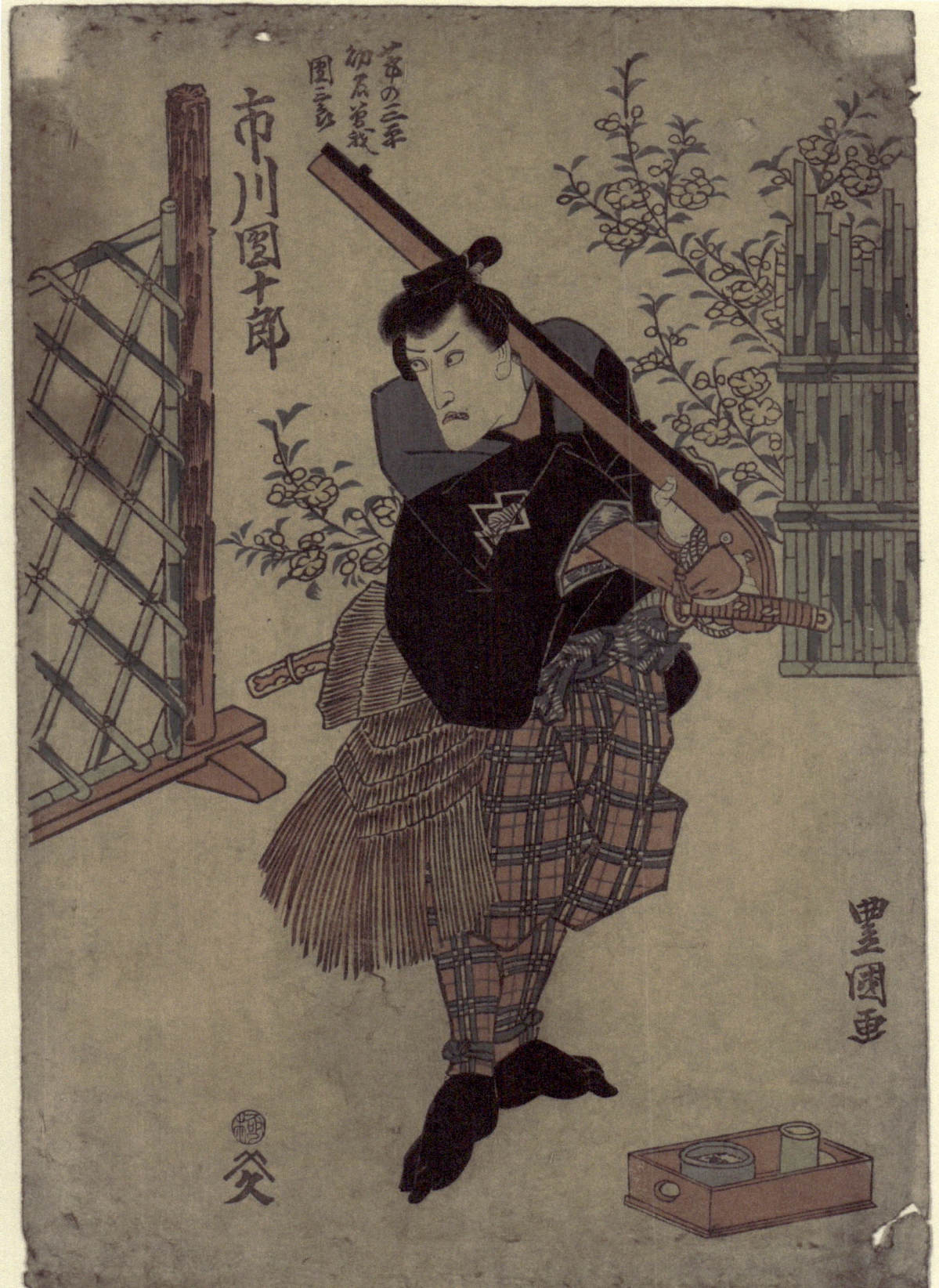

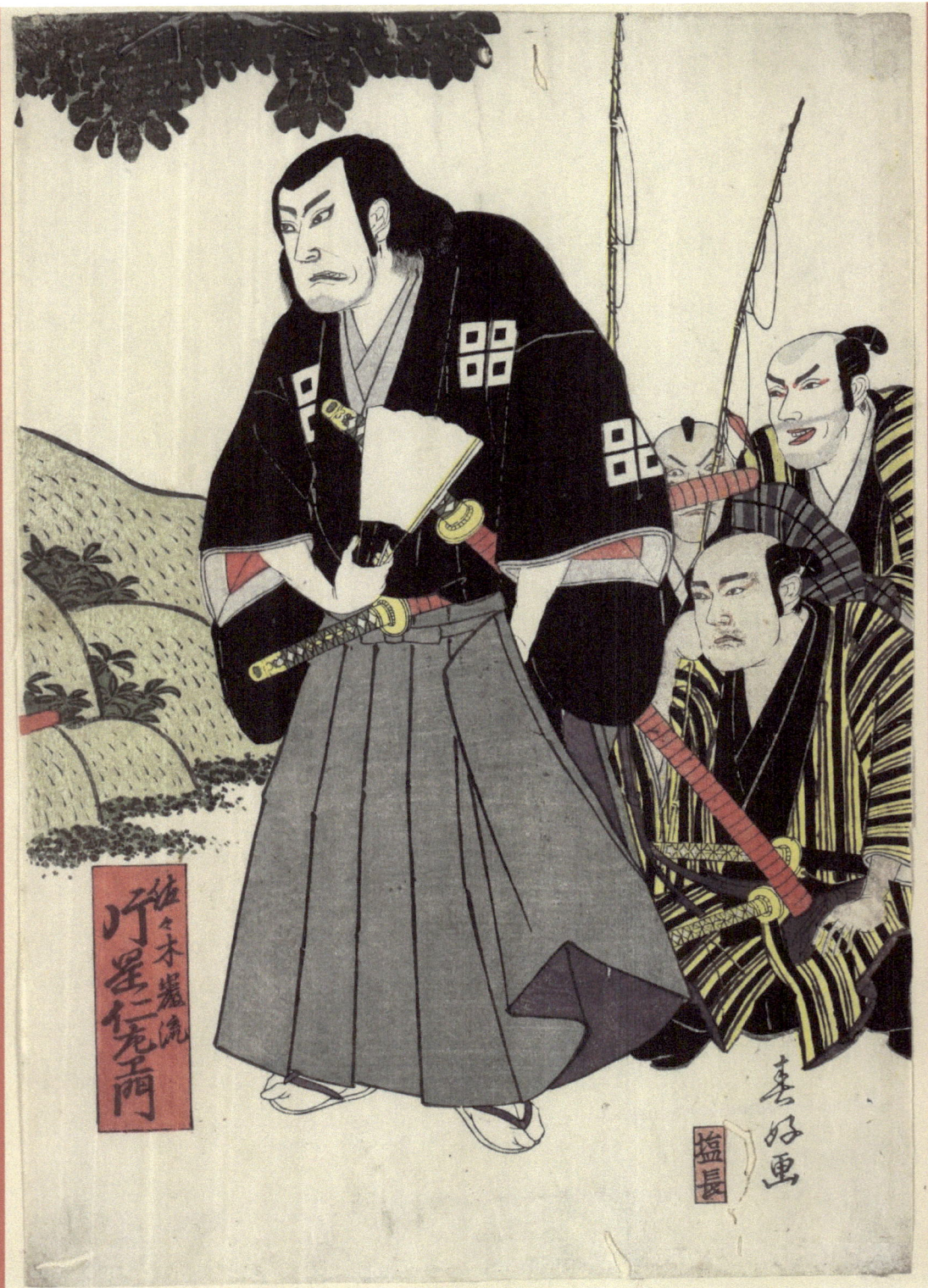

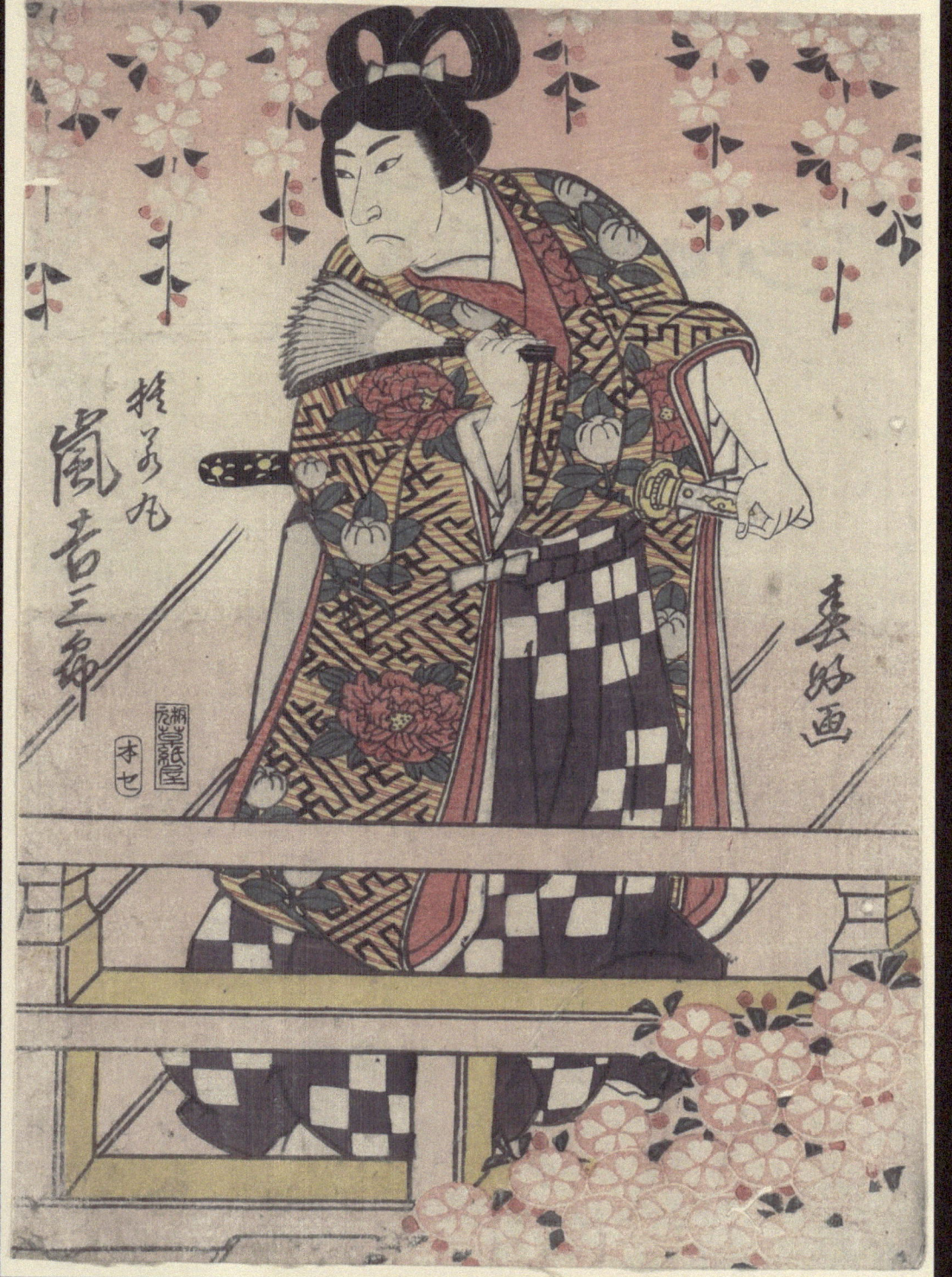

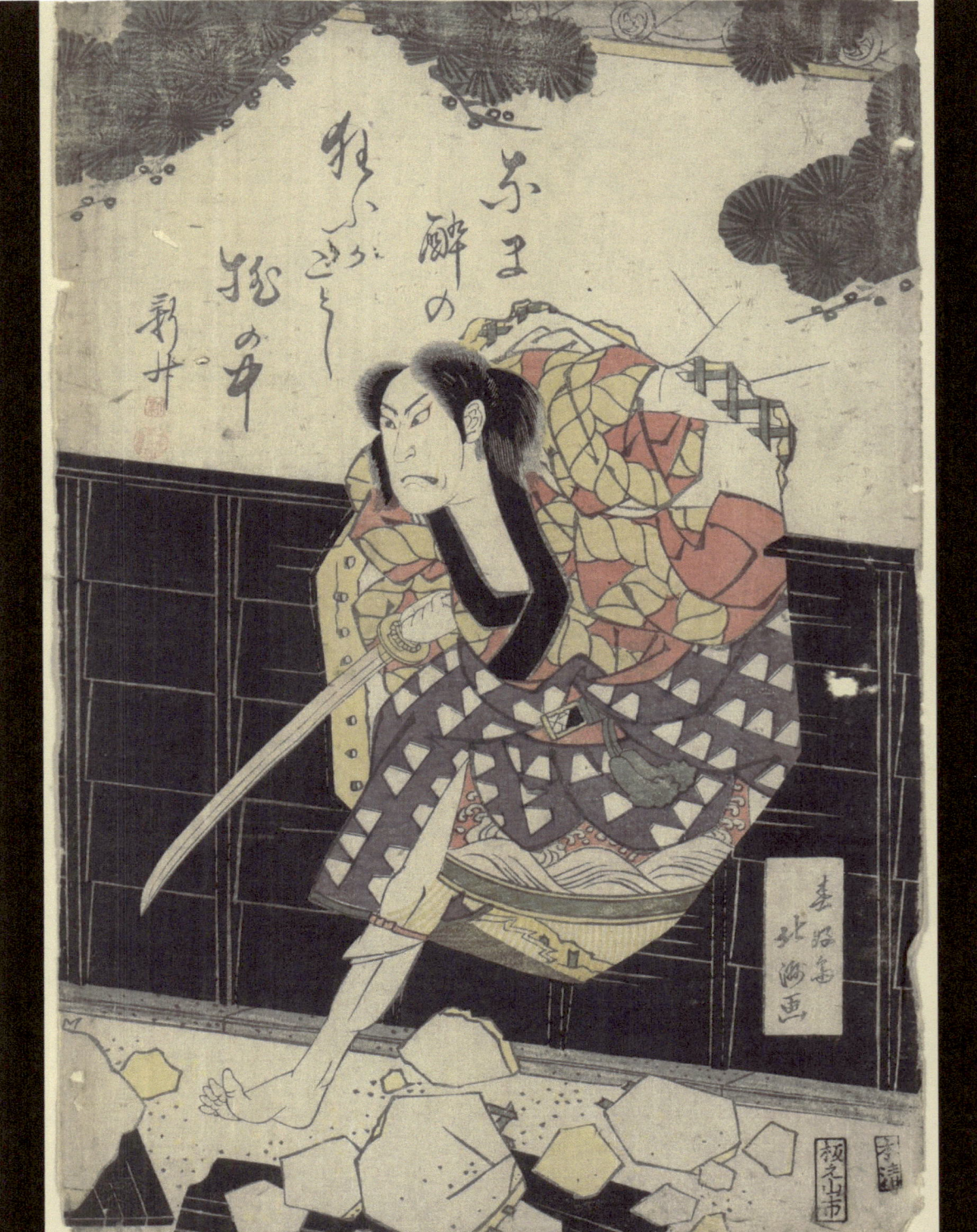

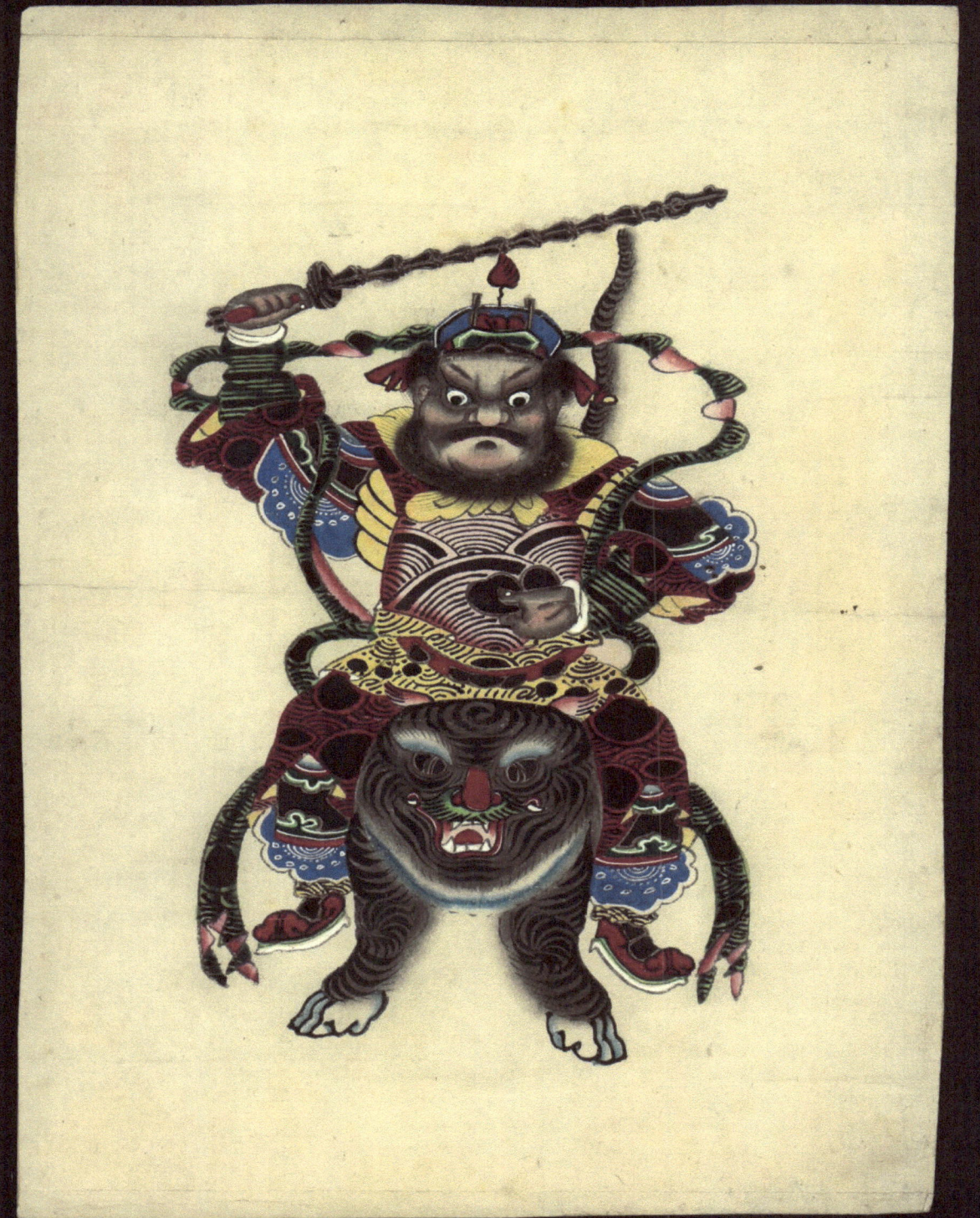

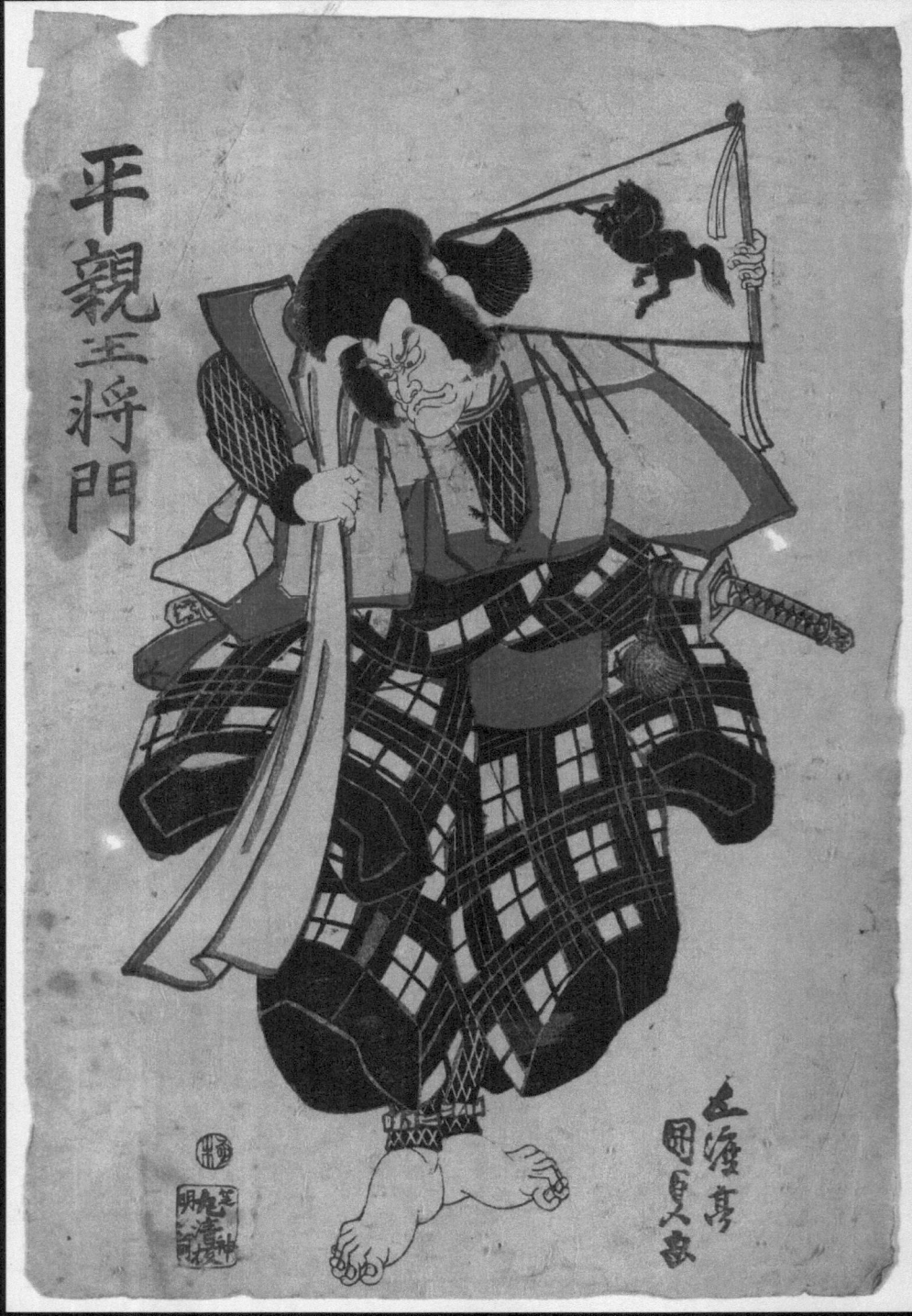

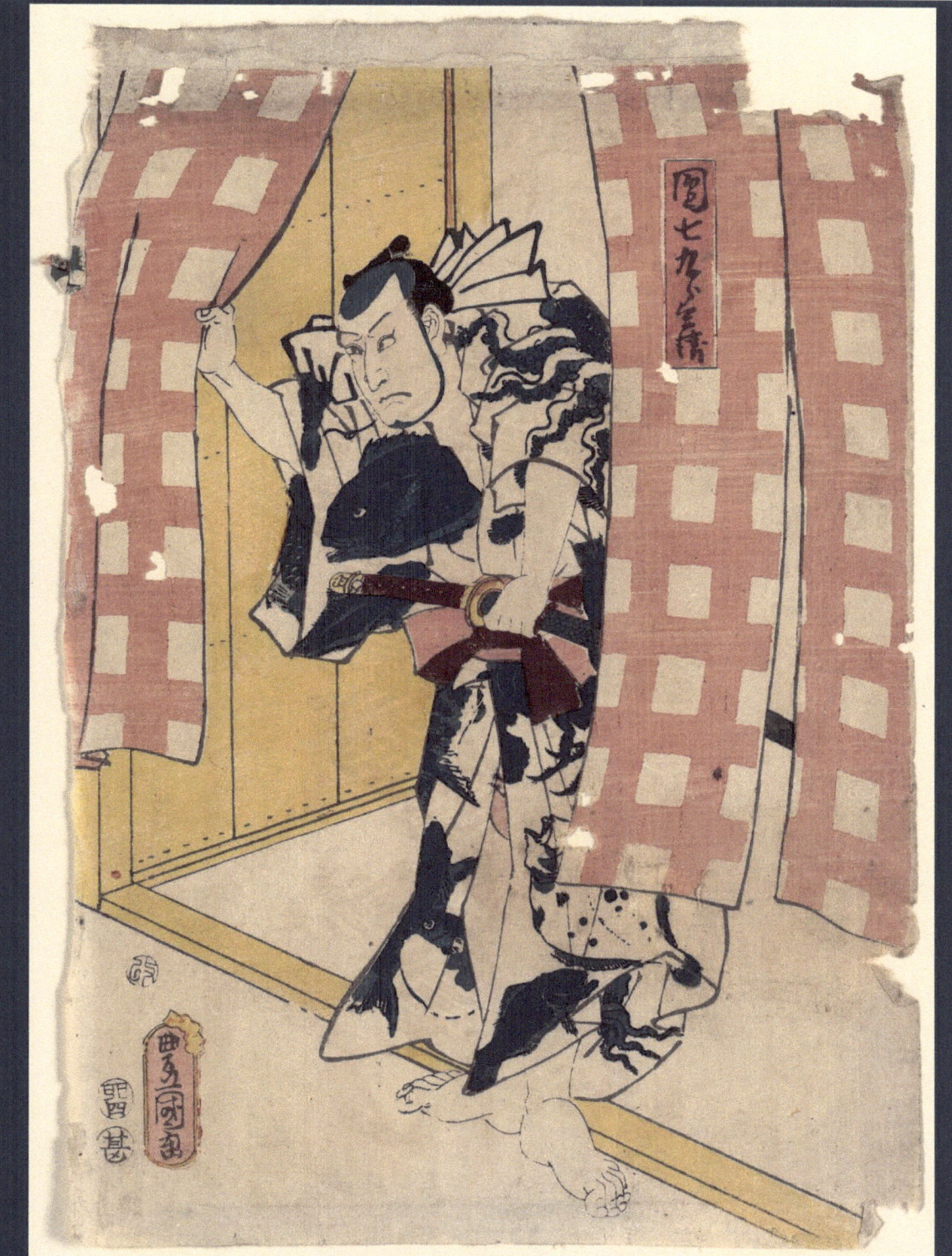

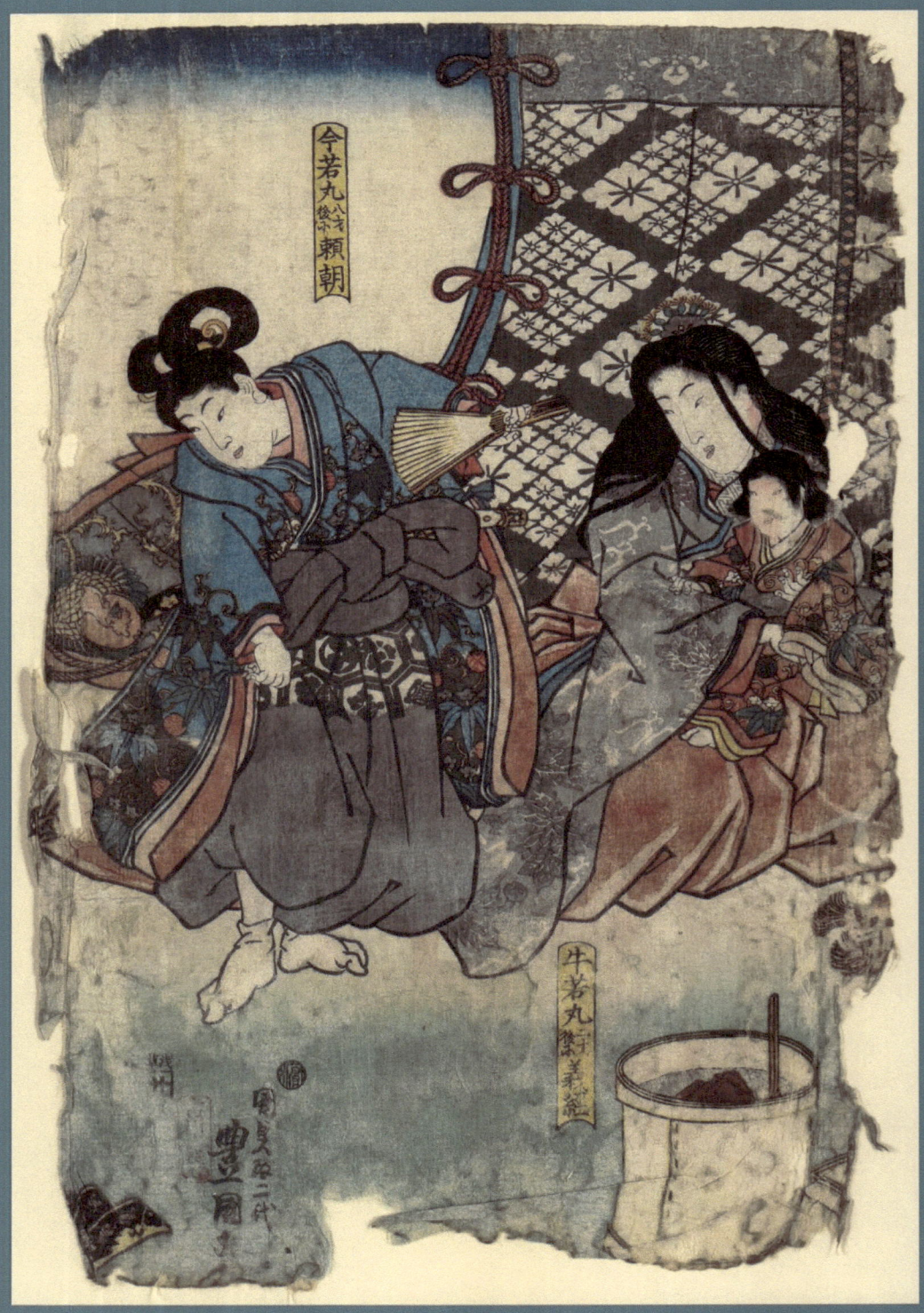

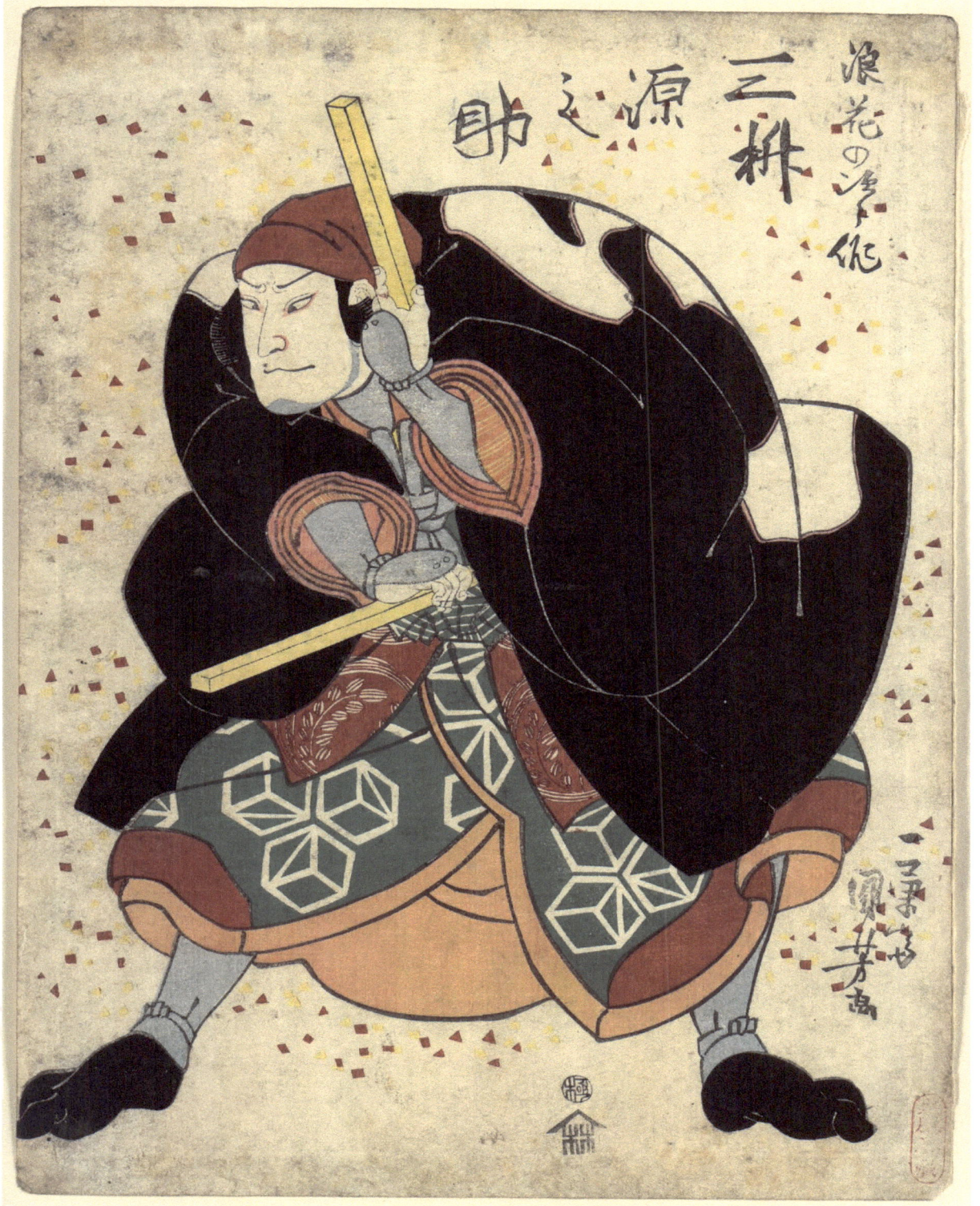

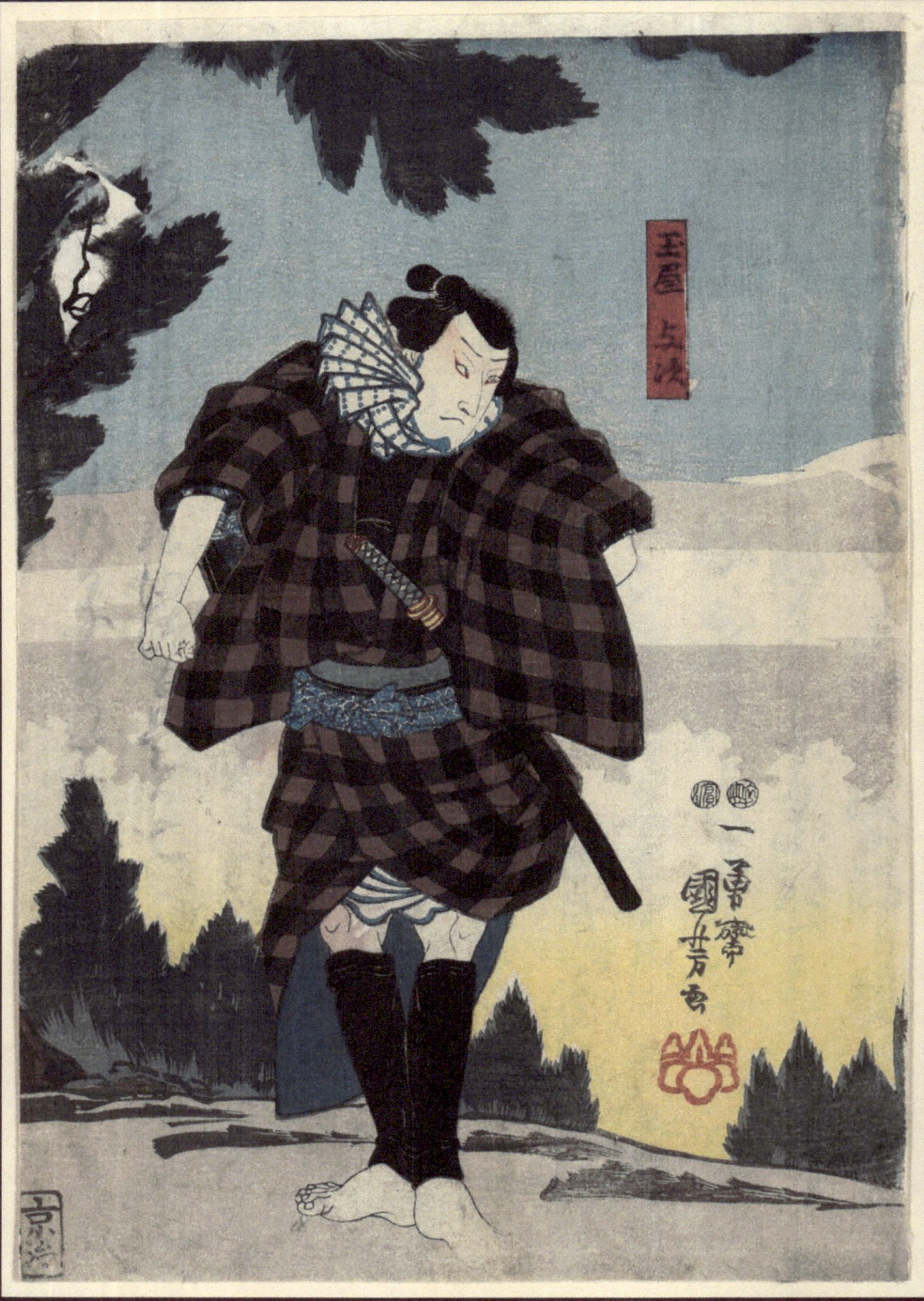

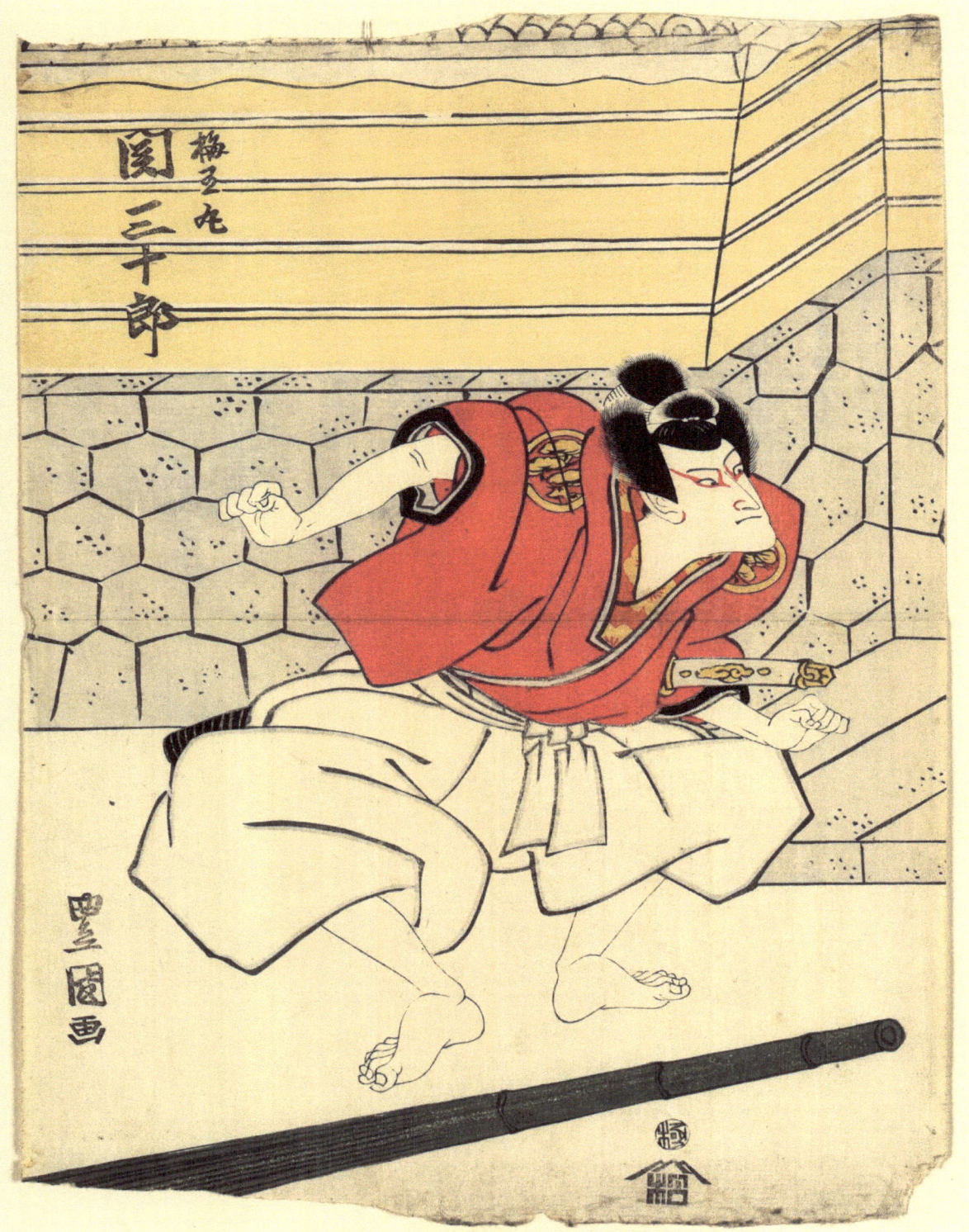

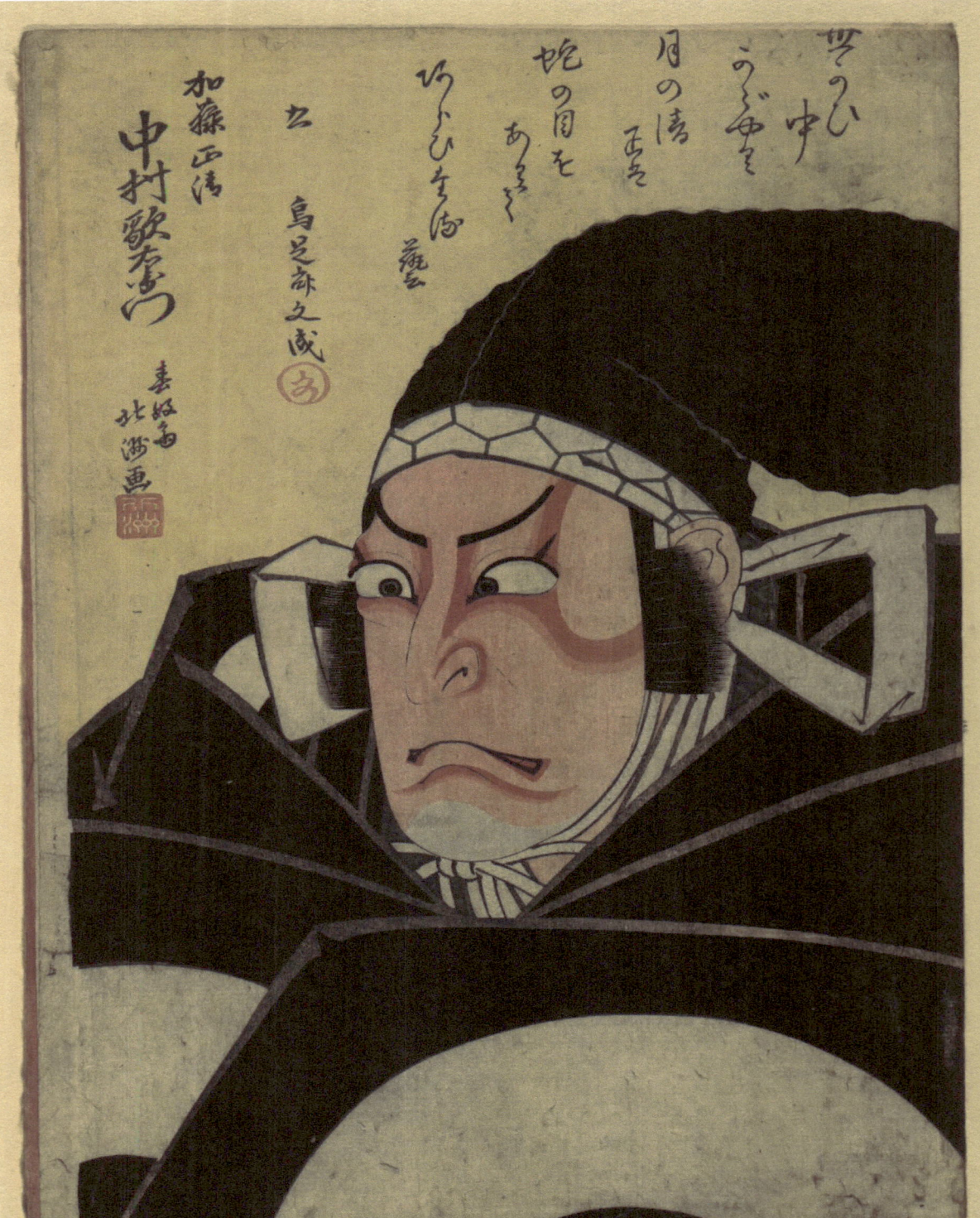

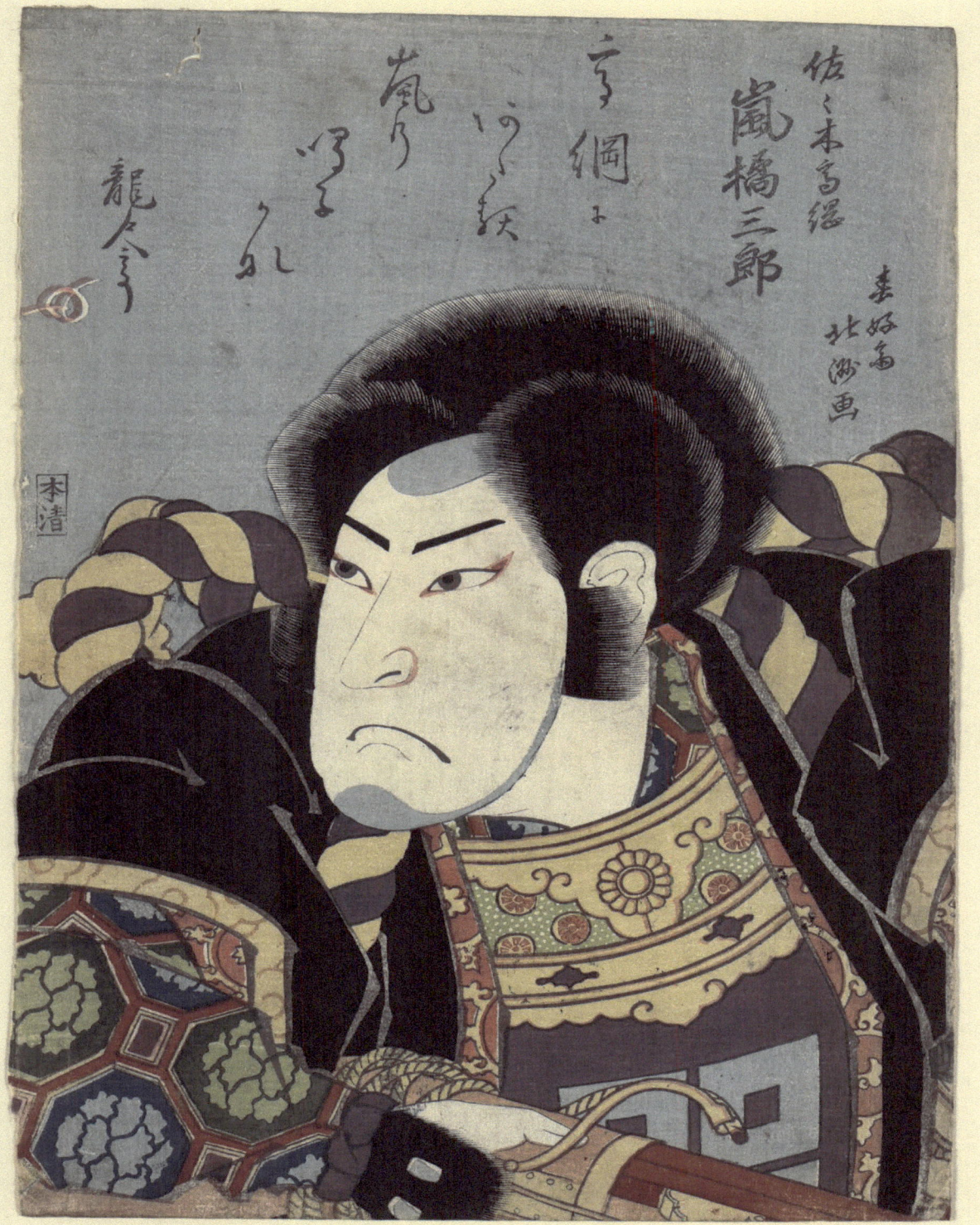

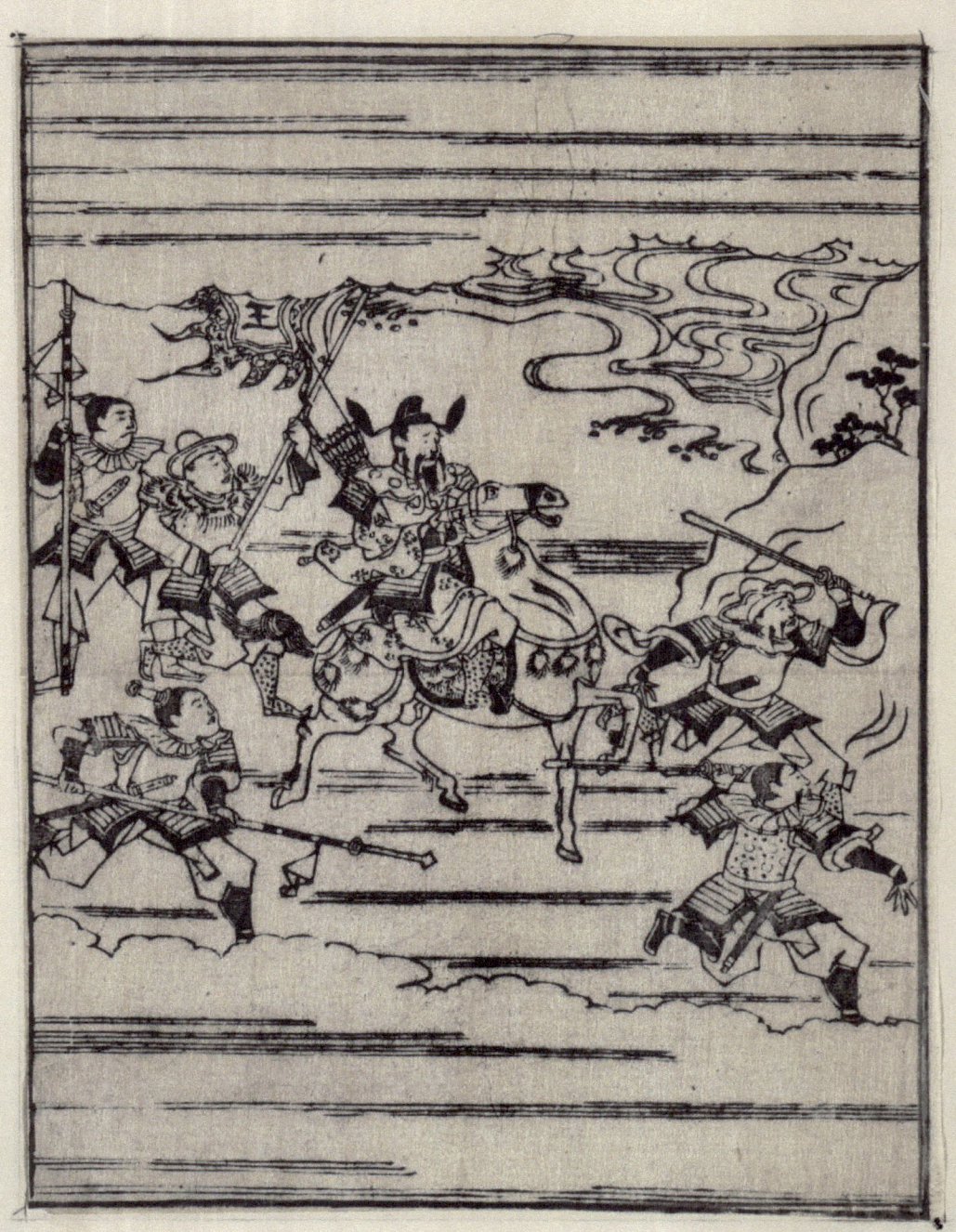

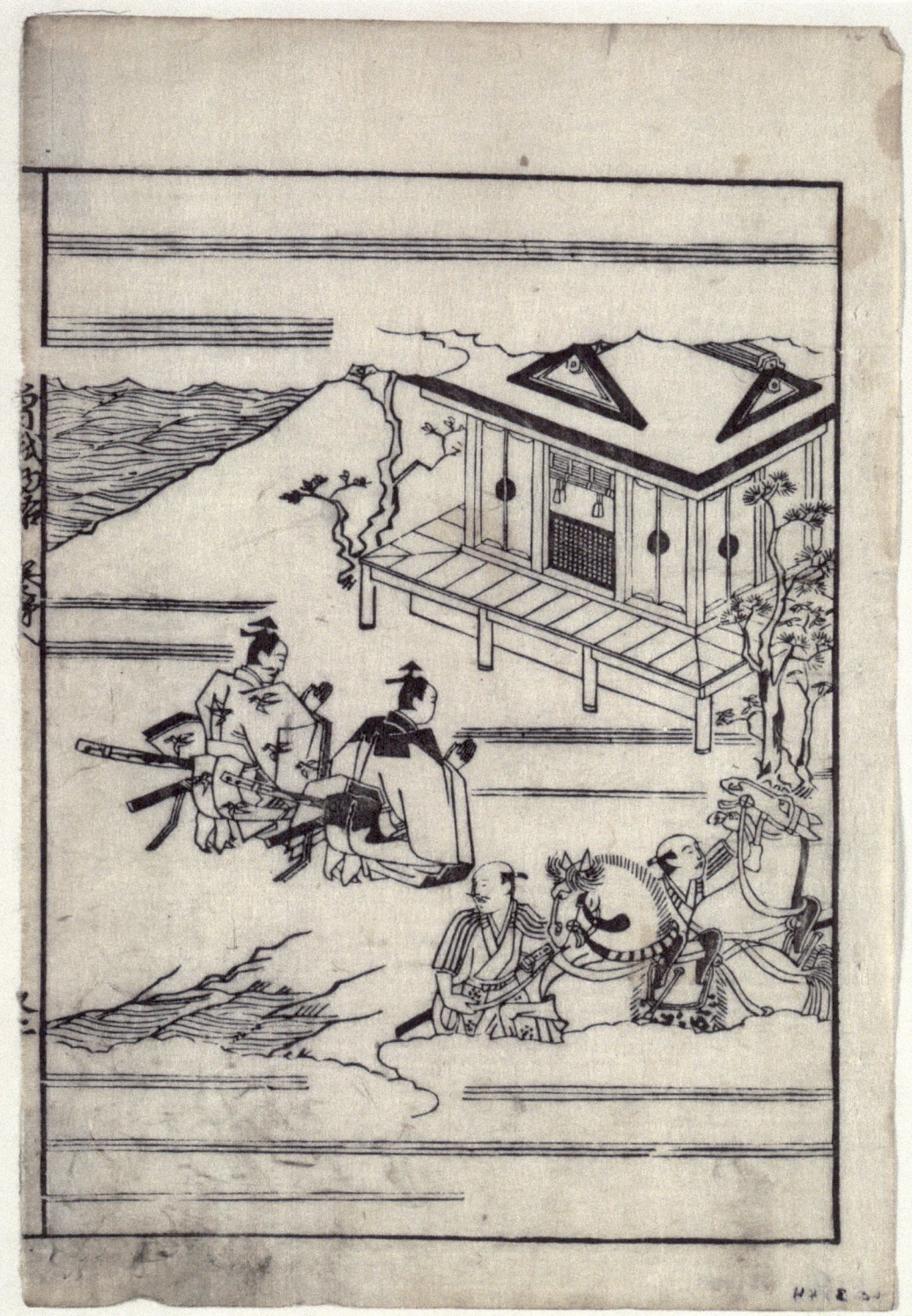

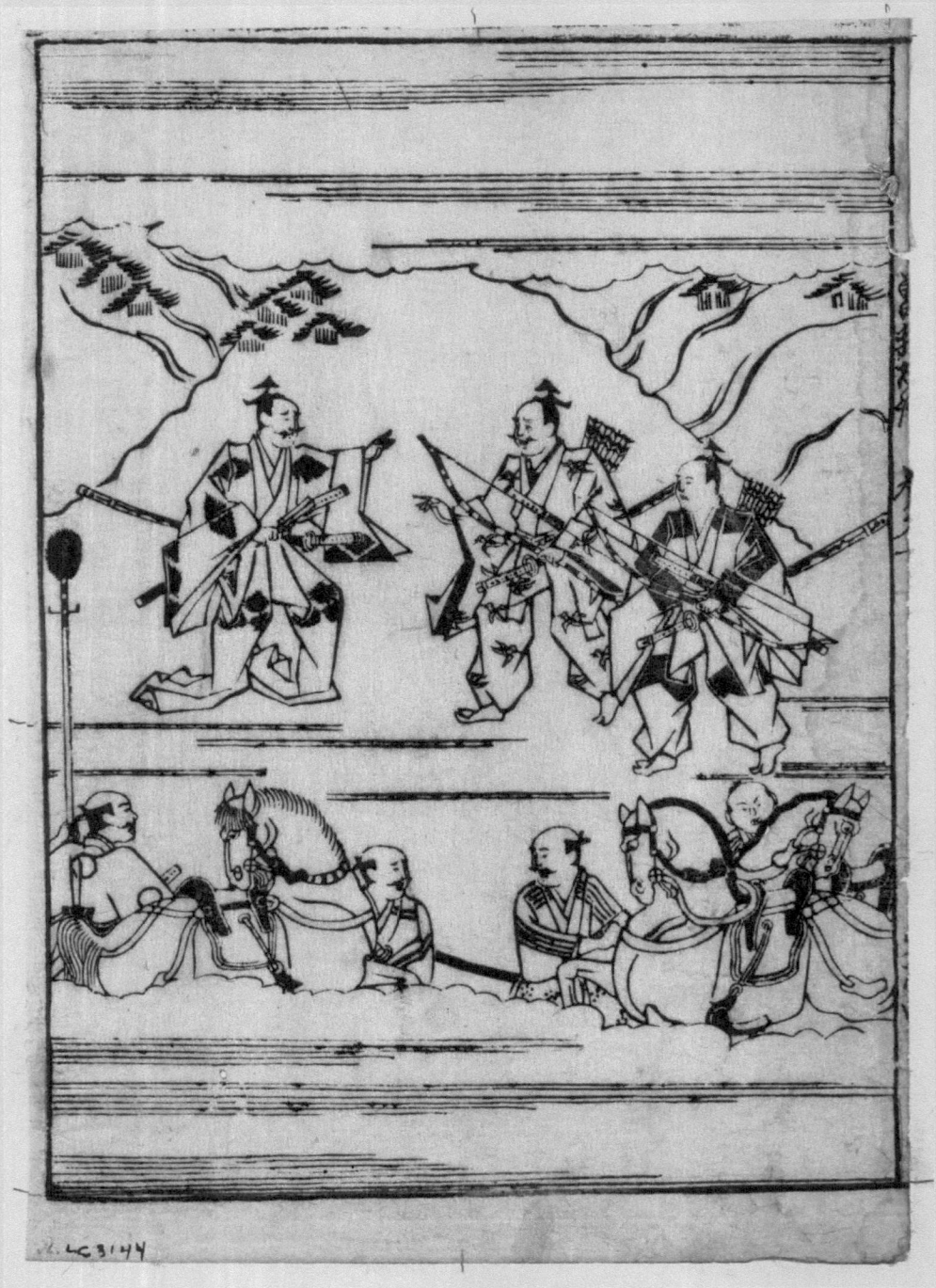

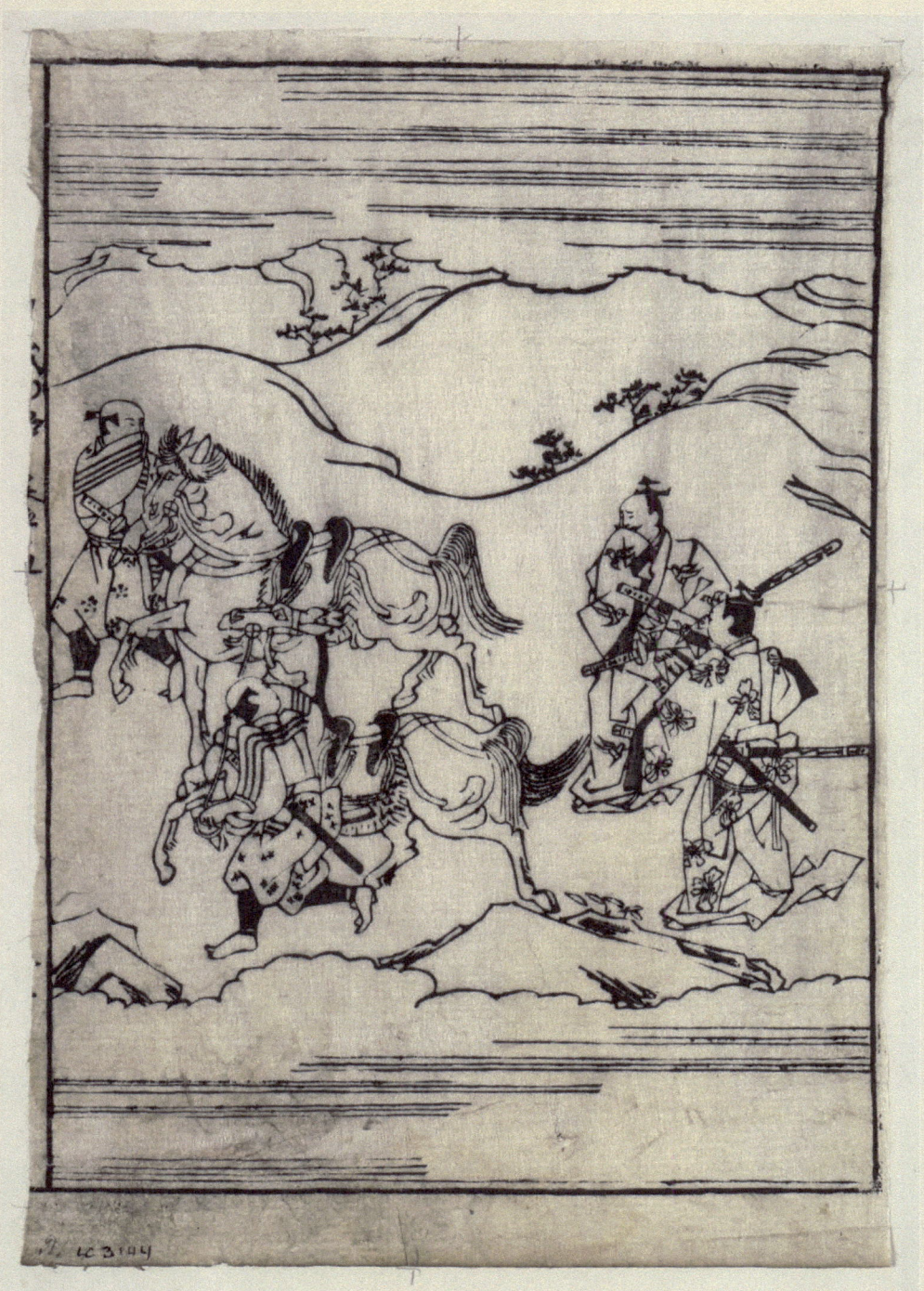

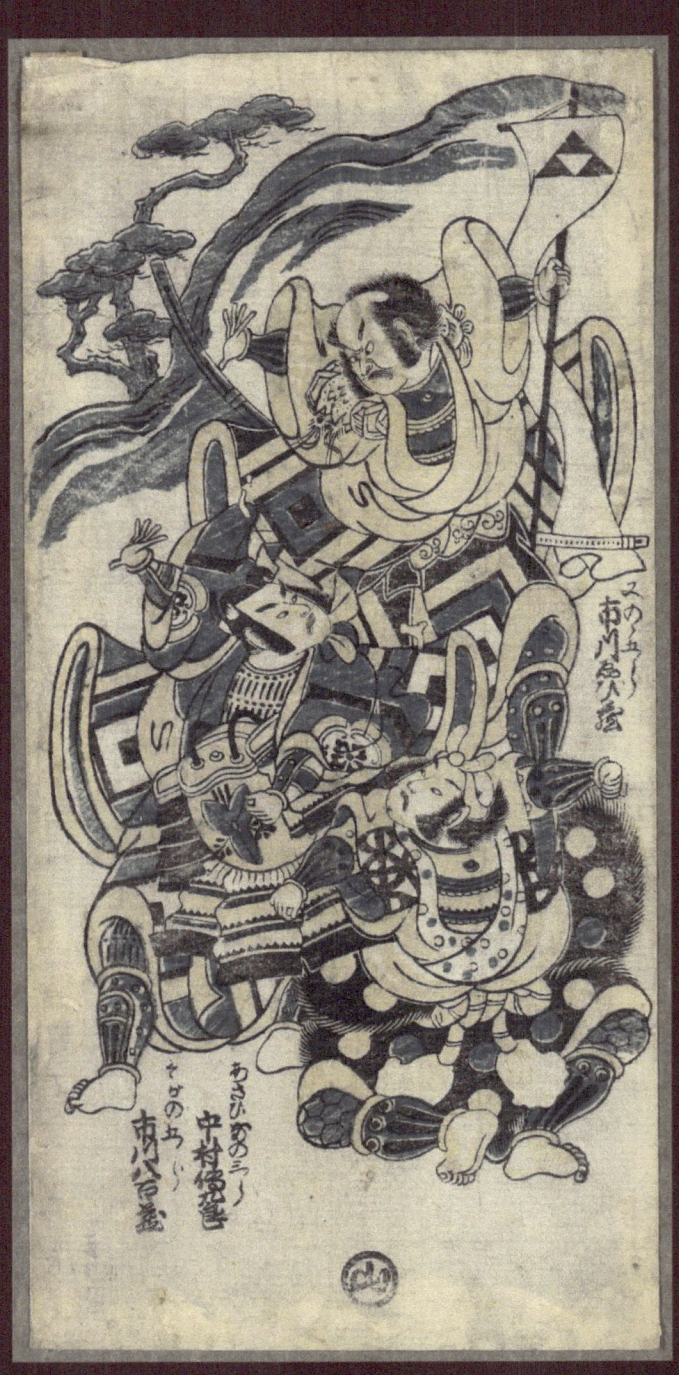

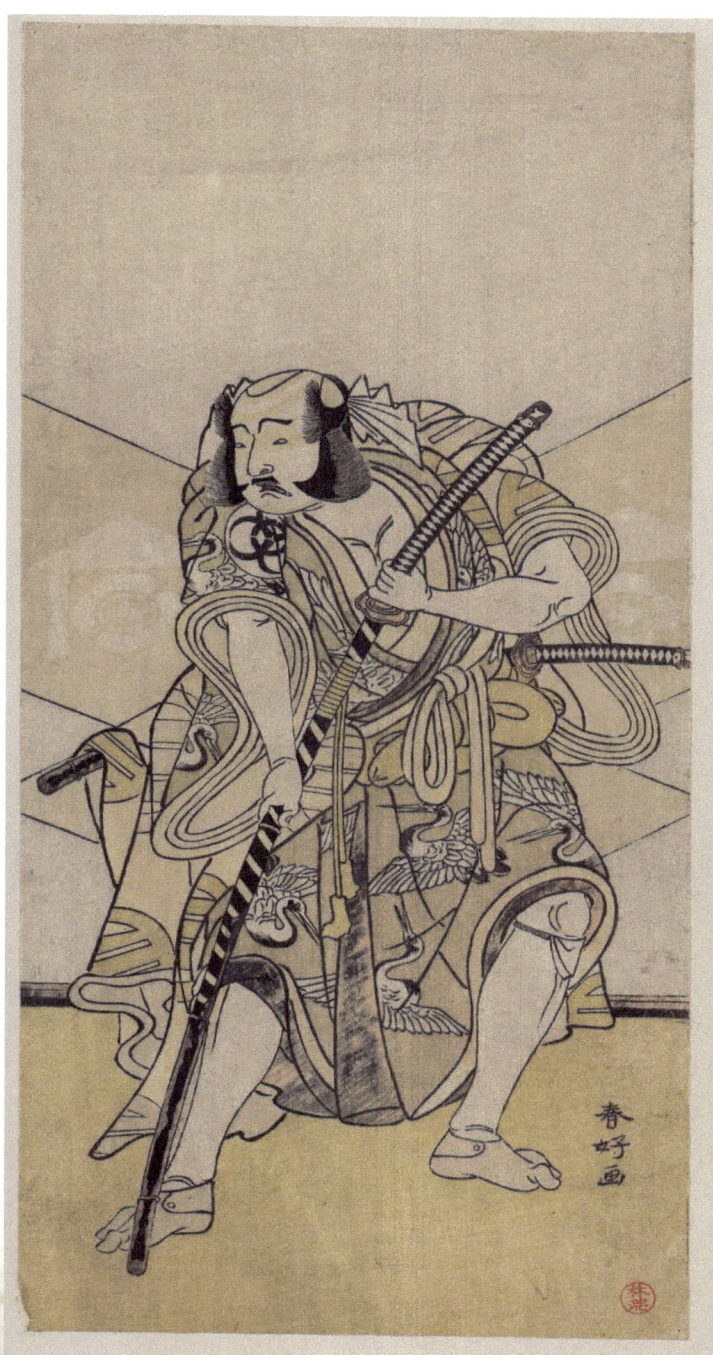

春好画

第五五八七號 春好筆 細絵一枚

四百十四
自五八二
至五九〇
丸揃

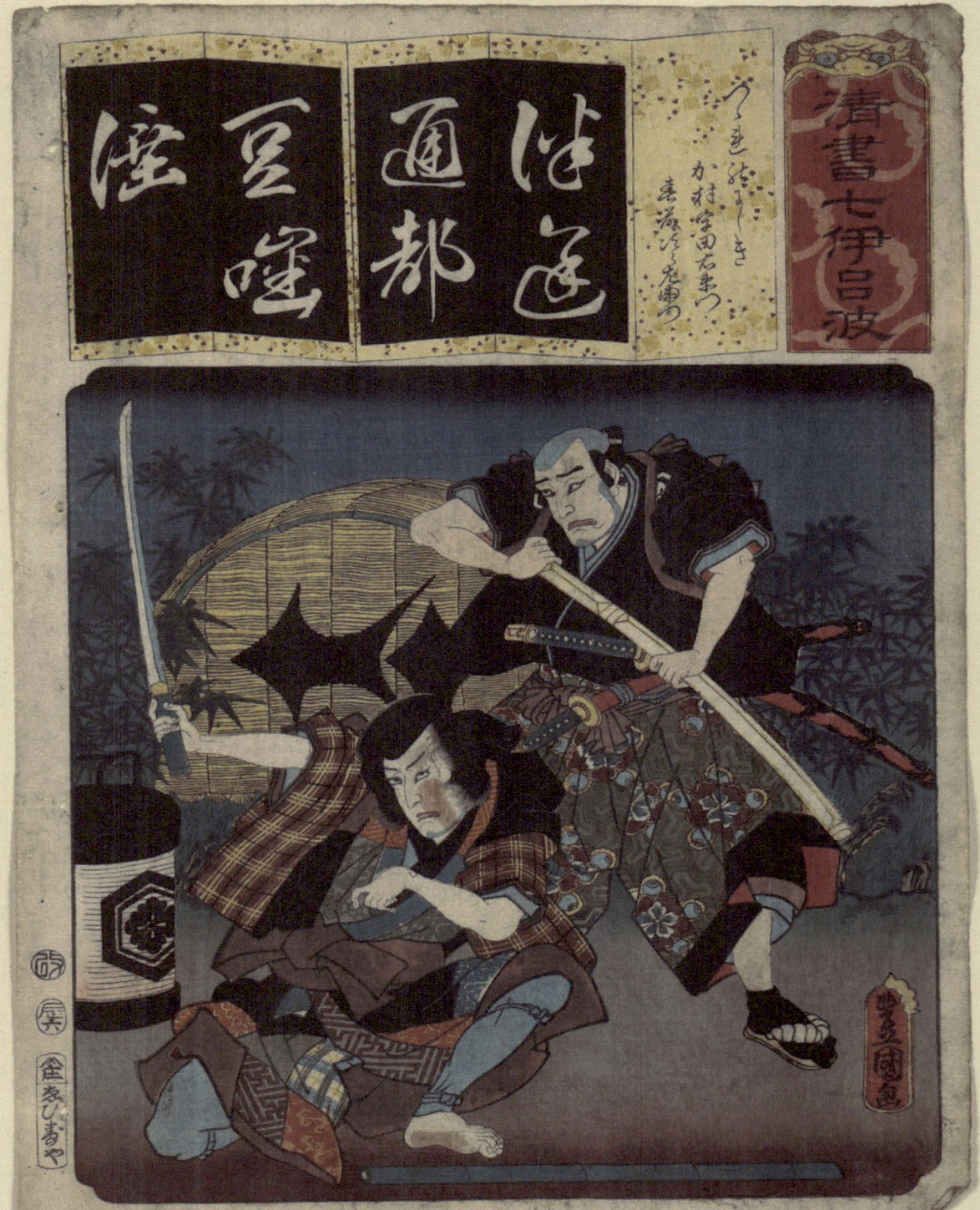

淫
豆喧

迺
通
郡

は
迺

清書七伊昌波

豊国
國

金ゑひ壽や